THE COMMUNIST NECESSITY

prolegomena to any future radical theory

J. Moufawad-Paul

KER
SPL
EBE
DEB
2014

The Communist Necessity: prolegomena to any future radical theory, by J. Moufawad-Paul

ISBN: 9781894946582

Copyright 2014 J. Moufawad-Paul
This edition copyright 2014 Kersplebedeb
first printing

> Kersplebedeb Publishing and Distribution
> CP 63560
> CCCP Van Horne
> Montreal, Quebec
> Canada H3W 3H8

> email: info@kersplebedeb.com
> web: www.kersplebedeb.com
>   www.leftwingbooks.net

Copies available from AK Press:

> AK Press
> 674-A 23rd St.
> Oakland, CA
> 94612

> phone: (510) 208-1700
> email: info@akpress.org
> web: akpress.org

Layout by J. Moufawad-Paul
Printed in Canada

COMMUNISM. We know it is a word to be used with caution. Not because, in the grand parade of words, it may no longer be very fashionable. But because our worst enemies have used it, and continue to do so. We insist. Certain words are like battlegrounds: their meaning, revolutionary or reactionary, is a victory, to be torn from the jaws of struggle.

The Invisible Committee

Yesterday we had nothing. Today we have two great historical experiences rich in lessons, experiences which are present, which are alive in us... We must insist that the fact that there have been two restorations does not deny that the revolution is the main trend. To deny this fact is a pipe dream of reactionaries because the world proletarian revolution continues to advance and we are a part of that advance. It is undeniable that the world proletarian revolution will demand the cost of bloodshed, but what does not demand the cost of blood in this world? We ourselves would not be here without the lives sacrificed by so many communists and revolutionaries.

Peruvian Communist Party

contents

overture

The leftist milieu in North America and Europe has now reached a point where the *movementism* of the late 1990s is approaching its limits. Following the collapse of the Eastern Bloc, China's descent into state capitalism, and the degeneration of abandoned and small socialist satellite states such as Cuba, the left at the privileged centres of global capitalism entered an era of chaos. Unwilling to accept that capitalism was the end of history, while at the same time believing that communism was a failed project, leftist organizations dealt with their confusion by either disintegrating or distancing themselves from the past. If the history of actually existing socialism had indeed proved itself to be a grand failure, then the only hope for the activist of the 1990s was to discover a new way of making revolution.

In those days, when fragile affinity groups embraced contingency and chaos in the hope that this disorganized method would somehow produce revolution, we imagined we were building something new. We were incapable of understanding that all we were doing was uncritically replicating past methods of organization that had already revealed their ineffectiveness prior to the spectacular failure of communism. We returned to anarchism without reflecting on the anarchist limits of the Spanish Revolution. We returned to disorganization without understanding all of those incoherent currents of socialism that had failed to build anything beyond utopian speculation. We refused to think through the problem of the state, forgetting the limits encountered by the communards in Paris. Incapable of understanding the precise meaning of the communist failure, we ended up repeating the past while imagining we were building something new.

The 1999 protests against the World Trade Organization in Seattle. The mobilization against the 2001 Free Trade Areas of the Americas Summit in Quebec City. The 2001 G8 protests in Genoa. These were the high-points of the anti-globalization movement. Together, along with other explosive moments of angry first world resistance, these struggles demonstrated a belief that innumerable and disconnected movements could topple capitalism, that their fractured efforts would intersect and amount to a critical breaking point. Eventually this practice would collide with the fact of highly organized and militarized states that, unlike the chaotic activists challenging the power of capitalism, were more than capable of pacifying discontent. This was movementism: the assumption that specific social movements, sometimes divided along lines of identity or interest, could reach a critical mass and together, without any of that Leninist nonsense, end capitalism.

By the time of the 2010 G20 Summit in Toronto this anti-capitalist methodology had already become a caricature of itself. The confrontations were echoed as tragedy or farce, there was a tired recognition that nothing would be accomplished, and the militants arrested were guilty only of demanding the right to protest. All of the high-points, if they were indeed high-points, of 1999 and 2001 were repeated in a tired and banal manner; the state remained unharmed, the activists resisting the state were punished. Before this farce, the coordinating committee of the 2010 demonstrations would absurdly maintain, on multiple email list-serves, that *we* were *winning*, and yet it could never explain what it meant by "we" nor did its claim about "winning" make very much sense when it was patently clear that a victory against the G20 would have to be more than a weekend of protests. Had we truly reached a point where victory was nothing more than a successful demonstration, where we simply succeeded in defending the liberal right to assembly? After all, it would be bizarre to assume that the people responsible for this triumphalist language actually believed that world imperialism would be defeated that weekend. They had already dampened their expectations, and when they spoke of winning they were simply demonstrating a defeatist acceptance of lowered stakes.

Those who refuse to recognize 2010 as a caricature, who continue to argue that this organizational form and strategy is the only way forward, are like the hippies of the 1960s: behind the times, focused on their "glory days" in the late 1990s and early 2000s, myopic in their inability to look beyond the boundaries of their time and space. They refuse to examine the past revolutions just as they refuse to examine the revolutionary movements of today, in those zones that they claim to defend against imperialism, that had never been enamoured with this movementist praxis. They are willing to settle for reformism and pretend that it is revolution, acting as if a successful defense of the right to assembly and the ability to make one's complaint heard are the only victories the movement can achieve.

In order to make sense of our impasse, we adopted new theories of organization, anything that did not resemble the failures of the past, desperately hoping we would find the holy grail that would make another world possible. We ventured out into theoretical terrains we believed were exciting because of the whirlwind jargon some theorists employed. We spoke of rhizomes, of bloom, of deterritorialization, of the multitude, of anything that did not completely resemble the old-fashioned jargon that stank of failure.

And yet our failures were not even world historical; we failed long before reaching those moments of grand failure that had disciplined us into adopting these alternative practices of rebellion. We were not even capable of replicating the failure of the Paris Commune, let alone the failures in Russia and China. We did nothing but protest, sometimes militantly agitating without any long-term plans, and fantasized that our activism was synonymous with revolution.

Meanwhile, even before we embarked upon this confused path of social movementism, people's wars were being launched in those zones we claimed to represent under the auspices of a theory we had assumed was dead. Incapable of looking beyond the boundaries of our own practice, we often refused to recognize these movements, cherry-picking those moments of resistance that resembled our own practices. Instead of the Sendero Luminoso we championed a particular narrative of the Zapatistas; instead of Nepal we focused on Venezuela; instead of the Naxalites we lauded the Arab Spring.

Possessing the privilege to ignore everything that did not resemble our supposedly new way of seeing the world, we dismissed anything that could teach us otherwise.

But now some of us—whose experiences of this banal failure have taught us that if another world is possible it is only possible by abandoning the methods promoted by the anti-globalization movement—are beginning to question the normative anarchism and movementism that we once treated as common sense. The movementist dream is crumbling; we are beginning to peer through its cracks. We are glimpsing the problem of revolutionary *necessity*: the need to organize in a manner that goes beyond the infantile methods of movementism.

Finally the name *communism* is being revived at the centres of capitalism as part of an effort to reclaim the revolutionary heritage we abandoned, although the revival is incomplete: there is a gap between *name* and *concept*; there is a refusal to recognize the communist revolutionary struggles that persisted in the global peripheries; there is an inability to grasp the dialectic of failure and success.

First, *the gap between name and concept*. While there is an ongoing project, amongst first world intellectuals and activists, to reclaim the name "communism" there are still only a few small steps made to reclaim the concepts this name once mobilized. This gap might demonstrate some confusion on the part of those who are dissatisfied with the anti-globalization variant of movementism but are still uncertain of how to free themselves from this morass. This gap is in part due to the way in which our understanding of communism is filtered through a first world experience of history and social struggle. Most importantly, however, this gap intersects with a gap between theory and practice.

Second, *the refusal to recognize contemporary communist revolutions.* Perhaps because of the first problem, we have a veritable lacuna of radical academic analysis when it comes to the experience of contemporary people's wars that have erupted and are still erupting outside of the imperialist centres. When we do not denounce these revolutionary movements according to various conservative or liberal narratives—they are "terrorists", "adventurists", "murderers", "nihilists", etc.—we simply pretend that they do not exist.

Third, *the inability to grasp the dialectic of failure and success.* As noted, common sense ideology has succeeded in presenting communism as a grand failure. Although we cannot escape the fact that past communist movements ultimately failed, this does not mean that they were not, at the same time, earth-shaking successes. If we can succeed in steering our way through the narrative of failure we will be able to understand the revolutionary truths hard-won by the successes that may transcend these failures—and it is here where communism's necessity will be discovered.

Those of us who have struggled without communist ideology for decades are only beginning to make sense of the meaning of the name we had once rejected; we are still trying to recapture our heritage.

chapter one:
21st century communism

Finally, after decades of post-modernism and capitalist triumphalism, it is no longer considered impolite for academics and popular intellectuals to speak the word *communism*. For there was a time, not long ago, when we would have been seen as uncouth, or at least anachronistic, if we were to declare fidelity to a term that certain intellectual fads had declared old-fashioned, totalizing, violent. Until recently, we could escape by referring to ourselves as marxist instead of communist, but only so long as we did not hyphenate our marxism with any of those suspicious names such as Lenin or Mao, those people and movements responsible for applying marxism and, in this application, declaring the word communism.

Marxism, though passé, was considered tooth-less because it was only a theory, whereas communism was its possibly catastrophic application. And those who preserved this theory in the academic universe were often those who would never dare bridge the gap between theory and practice, content only to teach and sing the praises of marxism but never speak of communism except when they spoke of failure. As it turned out, very little was needed to convince many academics and intellectuals to be marxists in theory rather than practice: the job security of tenure, liberal rights such as freedom of speech, and publication contracts.

In this context, those intellectuals who refused to abandon political practice but who could not stomach the failed name of communism would fall back onto the more innocuous-sounding *socialism* when they sought a label for their activities. A term that was once synonymous with communism, but that through the experience of the great revolutions of the 20th century had come to mean something altogether different, became a fall-back definition for those marxists who would not remain content with inaction. This was a retreat, of sorts, back into a "pure" marxism—before Lenin—where concepts that should have been irrevocably transformed by world historical revolutions were reordered to resume their germinal status; a retreat from history, a retreat from the development of revolutionary concepts won through class struggle.

By the dawn of the 21st century it had become vogue for the more daring first world marxist academics and intellectual partisans to speak of a "21st Century Socialism" as if they were identifying a new revolutionary moment. More than one book was written with this catch-phrase embedded somewhere in its title or subtitle, more than one speaker at a mainstream demonstration bandied it about, and yet there was generally no consensus regarding its meaning. Some imagined that this new socialism was emerging in the movementist tides of the anti-globalization protests that began in Seattle; others thought it was happening in the jungles of Mexico with the Zapatistas [EZLN]; others would eventually ascribe it to Chavez's Venezuela or some other left populist phenomenon in the Americas. Just what made this "21st Century Socialism" new or a product of the 21st century, though, was rather unclear despite all attempts to make it seem apparent; it was more of a branding than anything else, an attempt to mobilize other and successive maxims—"another world is possible," "we are everywhere," "the coming insurrection"—that were always little more than slogans. And this nebulous fad avoided speaking of communism, of anything that would remind us of those significant decades in the 20th century that were seen as abject failure. This was the 21st century, after all, and we would be old-fashioned and out of touch if we spoke of those moments without melancholia.

But now, in the past three or four years, there has been a resurgence of the name that was banned, the name we were told was obsolete, from the same quarters where it had been declared anathema. Now we have academics and popular intellectuals speaking of communist hypotheses, communist horizons, and communist possibilities. What was once taboo in these spaces is now being pronounced openly and these pronouncements are not destroying the careers of those who make them. Quite the opposite, in fact: now some careers are being made by declaring fidelity to the name that was once banned.

At the same time, however, this new intellectual trend of declaring the name communism cannot break from the previous period of fearfulness and so shares all of the defects and nebulous speculations of the screeds to 21st Century Socialism. In many ways this is just a substitution of one term for another, apparently more edgy because it now chooses to speak the name that was once forbidden. While it is true that there is an excitement in reclaiming a word that once frightened the capitalist order, this truth is toothless if it is nothing more than a name.

Some would speak of communism as an idea or hypothesis that existed for thousands of years, nearly wrenching it from those generations who died in innumerable brave attempts to make it the watch-word of the oppressed in the 20th century. In this sense the word was dehistoricized, transformed into a Platonic form, and those instances of fear and trembling where it was elevated to great heights—heights, true, from which it would fall—were treated as ruptured moments to be remembered only for their nostalgic importance.[1]

Others would speak of communism as a far-off horizon, some distant point we could only glimpse, and thus more of an inborn desire for another and possible world. A dream communism, something we might approach if we only have enough faith in disorganized and rebellious movements to take us there on directionless tides. A communism across a great ocean, hiding like the lost island of Atlantis.[2]

Still others speak of the word as a name that must be reclaimed because it makes the ruling classes tremble. We must renew this name, we are told, because it is correct to veil ourselves in the terminology our enemy despises—as if revolutionary action is a monstrous mask that will scare capitalism into retreat. At the same time we are also told that renewing those traditions that provided us with this name,

---

1. Alain Badiou's concept of the "communist hypothesis" and Slavoj Zizek's concept of "the idea of communism" represent this trend.

2. Jodi Dean's concept of the "communist horizon", taken from Bruno Bosteel's book *The Actuality of Communism* (London: Verso, 2011) is paradigmatic of this trend.

that handed us an important concept through great sacrifice, should be avoided. "Communization" rather than the revolutionary communism of the past is the goal.[3] Again, this is the 21st century and we are supposed to find a new method; even if it must share its name with past movements, we are told that we cannot take anything from this past because this past was only, and can only ever be, tragic.

Despite a return to the name communism there still appears to be a refusal to accept everything this name was supposed to mean—because we were told it meant mass murder, totalitarianism, and most importantly failure. We want to reclaim it, we might even want to argue against the cold war discourse that speaks of mass murder and totalitarianism just to set the record straight, but we have been convinced that the catastrophe of 20th century communism means we must start anew, that we can learn nothing from the past except to ignore this past altogether.

Perhaps this refusal to reclaim communism in more than name is due to the "end of history" proclaimed when the Soviet Union collapsed, when capitalists imagined they were finally triumphant

---

3. Tiqqun, the Invisible Committee, Endnotes, Théorie Communiste, and various anarcho-communist and autonomist individuals and collectives represent this trend.

and wanted to convince us that class struggle was antiquated. Here began a discourse about communism—a discourse evinced by the rise of postmodern theory—where we were taught that to even speak the name communism was backwards, and that we should just accept that capitalism was "the best of the worst." In this context, it is not surprising that the first academic attempts to reclaim the word are tentative. Better to hedge our bets and remake communism than speak more precisely of a theoretical tradition supposedly concluded when capitalist victory closed that historical chapter.

And yet, despite this supposed "end of history", communism as a revolutionary tradition never did go away. For though it might seem daring for academics and popular intellectuals at the centres of global capitalism to reclaim the word, communism has remained a vital necessity for individuals and movements living at the margins of both the world system and acceptable discourse. At the global centres communists generally hid themselves within the labour and student movements, grudgingly accepted the terminology of *socialism*, and often practiced a fearful blanquism. At the peripheries, however, there are communists who have openly proclaimed a revolutionary communism from the very moment capitalism was declaring itself victorious: the Peruvian Communist Party [PCP] launched a people's war in the 1980s; the Communist Party of

Nepal (Maoist) [CPN(Maoist)] launched a people's war in the late 1990s; the Communist Party of India (Maoist) [CPI(Maoist)] is engaged in a people's war now; the Communist (Maoist) Party of Afghanistan [CmPA] is planning on launching its own people's war in the near future; the Communist Party of the Philippines [CPP] has been carrying out its people's war, with setbacks and re-initiations, for some time now. In these spaces outside of the academic and intellectual arena—an arena where our daringness is measured by reclaiming only a name—communism remains a live option in the most forceful and momentous sense. It has not gone away, it is not just a name upon which a radical academic career can be built.

So while it might seem, for those of us who live at the centres of capitalism, as if communism has been absent for decades and is only now being reclaimed by our daring new theorists, the fact is that this is simply a mirage: communism did not bow off the historical stage, it is not only now being renewed by Slavoj Zizek, Alain Badiou, Jodi Dean, and whoever else has re-pronounced the word here at the centres of capitalism. The fact is that it renewed itself again, in a revolutionary sense, in the 1980s just when capitalism was proclaiming the death of communism and the end of history. But many of us who live in the global metropoles missed this event, or even continue to plead ignorance, content to imagine that we can remake history here. That we can reinvent the meaning of communism as we please, ignoring those revolutionary movements that, if we have learned anything from Marx, are responsible for making history. Movements that have the most obvious fidelity to the name and that express this name, even in failed revolutions, are better than our tentative attempts to merely reclaim and rearticulate a word.

The word *communism* remains and will always be re-proclaimed and reasserted as long as capitalism remains. More than a hypothesis or horizon, communism is a *necessity* that will never cease being a necessity for the duration of capitalism's hegemony; all successes and failures need to be appreciated and even claimed in this context. If we understand communism as a necessity we can comprehend not only the need for its renewal and re-proclamation, but why it cannot simply actualize itself outside of history according to transhistorical hypotheses and nebulous future horizons. We must speak of a necessary communism grounded in the unfolding of history, a communism that is simultaneously in continuity with and in rupture from the past, a communism that is always a *new return*.

against utopianism

To speak of renewing communism as a necessity is to begin from that point, first opened by Marx and Engels, where the tradition of anti-capitalism was torn from its utopian basis. As Engels wrote in *Anti-Duhring*, that diatribe which Marx believed was the best summation of their theory to date:

> if the whole of modern society is not to perish, a revolution in the mode of production and distribution must take place, a revolution which will put an end to all class distinctions. On this tangible, material fact, which is impressing itself in a more or less clear form, but with insuperable necessity, on the minds of the exploited proletarians—on this fact, and not on the conceptions of justice and injustice held by an armchair philosopher, is modern socialism's confidence in victory founded.[4]

4. Friedrich Engels, *Anti-Duhring* (New York: International Publishers, 1987), 146. Of course, at the point in history when Engels used the term "modern socialism" he meant "scientific" socialism—which is to say communism. For it is not until Marxism-Leninism that the concepts of socialism and communism are disentangled; until then, there was still some semantic confusion. Indeed, up until the great betrayal of the Social Democratic Party of Germany [SPD], whose founders had known Engels, it was still considered normative to use the

Engels' argument would later be simplified, by Rosa Luxemburg, to mean *socialism or barbarism*. That is: either we embrace the possibility of a socialist revolution that could establish communism or we accept that capitalism is the end of history and thus the fact of barbarism—that "modern society is to perish." Communism, then, is a necessity because otherwise capitalism, due to its intrinsic logic, will devour existence.

And it is senseless to speak of communist horizons in any other way. For what other reason is there to desire a better world beyond the limits of capitalism? Because capitalism is *mean*, *evil*, *immoral*—because we don't like it? These are, as Engels was quick to note at the end of the nineteenth century, the complaints of armchair philosophers: abstract moral theorizing cannot escape the problem of competing class morality, and those who attempt to establish a concrete morality that is universal, even when they are not pulled back into the terrain

---

term "social democracy" as a synonym for both socialism and communism; it is only with this party's betrayal—first with Eduard Bernstein and then with Karl Kautsky—that "social democracy" became associated with social reform. Similarly, it was only after Lenin that the term "socialism" became the theoretical designation of the dictatorship of the proletariat. Theoretical terminology was ironed out over the course of revolution and, if we believe that revolution is the locomotive of history, we cannot go back to a pure marxism before the first world historical, communist-led revolution in Russia.

of abstract morality, are still incapable of producing revolution. Such justifications do not provide a reason to transcend capitalism—to speak of any horizon—for they are most often caught within a dialogue of competing moralities: the morality of the oppressor is to continue oppressing; the morality of the oppressed is to revolt. The only reason why the latter is superior to the former is a reason that must come from outside of this debate: the necessity of revolution due to the fact that the position of the former is, in the last instance, contingent upon the annihilation of the basis of existence. And that the latter—the exploited, the oppressed, the wretched of the earth—make history. Communism, then, is more than an ethical necessity: it is an historical and material necessity.

But it is precisely this point of necessity that recent talk of communism, which speaks of hypotheses and horizons, seems to evade. To claim that "another world is possible," after all, is not the same as claiming that another world is necessary. (Or, more accurately, that even this world is unsustainable as it exists now; another world, then, becomes necessary if we are to survive and flourish as a species.) Instead we speak of the importance of a transhistorical hypothesis, or the theoretical significance of a world somewhere over the rainbow. Hence the immediacy of the communist project—that which speaks to the immanence of revolution—is often ignored.

To speak of a communist necessity is to speak precisely of the need for revolution: if we claim that communism is an immediate need — a necessity produced by the logic of capitalism as Engels suggests — then we should be led to thinking through the necessary steps that would end capitalism and bring communism into being. A hypothesis is simply a philosophical quandary, a horizon is little more than a fantasy, a possibility is a useful way of recognizing that the current reality may not be eternal, but a necessity is so much more. Communism is necessary, a material need; this tells us what it means to declare fidelity to the name communism.

To dodge the question of necessity is to dodge the need for revolution. To take the question of communism and place it in the stark framework Engels emphasized in *Anti-Duhring*, though, might not seem as sexy as to speak of hypotheses and horizons. Why bother returning to a supposedly "scientific" statement made by Engels at the end of the 19th century, after all, when the 21st century is upon us and we need to repopularize communism without recourse to some stodgy and apparently old-fashioned way of looking at the world? But now, with the annihilation of the entire ecosystem an immediate possibility because of the logic of capitalism, Engels' framing of the question of necessity should be even more striking. The question *socialism or barbarism?* is not a philosophical thought experiment but a momentous demand.

The dream of a possible horizon does nothing to answer the immediacy of this question because it fails to address the problem of necessity. Dreams are like this: fantasies projected upon the future that tend to side-step those messy real world events where there were significant attempts to build the content of these dreams. The thing about real life, unfortunately, is that it never identically resembles the dream. Thus, instead of dreaming about horizons it is better to recognize that we are currently caught in the dream of capitalism as lucid dreamers in a terrible nightmare; when we recognize that we are in a nightmare, it is *waking* that becomes a necessity rather than subordinating ourselves to another fantasy.

And yet to speak of communism as something other than a necessity is an easy way to reclaim the word without reclaiming anything but a vague idea behind the word. It is to intentionally ignore what is needed, in a very concrete and material sense, to bring communism into being. Hypotheses are things that can be worked out, that require academic investigation; horizons are points of existence out of sight; possibilities are open questions. Necessities, however, demand our immediate attention and mobilize practice. When the movements behind the two great but unsuccessful world historical revolutions of the 20th century recognized that communism was a visceral necessity, they developed theories that spoke to this necessity and that, despite their eventual failures, brought us closer to the possibility, to recognizing the hypothesis, to breaching the horizon.

The recognition of the necessity for communist revolution, first in Russia and then in China, produced a certain level of revolutionary success that could only lead to the encounter of other necessities. If anything, these moments, whatever their short-comings, should remind us of the importance of communism and its necessity; we should not hide from these failures, attempt to side-step them by a vague rearticulation of the terminology, or refuse to grasp that they were also successes. If we are to learn from the past through the lens of the necessity of making revolution, then we need to do so with an honesty that treats the practice of making communism as an historical argument.

the problem of movementism

All of this new talk about communism that avoids the necessity of actually bringing communism into being demonstrates a fear of the very name communism. In this context one can be a communist in theory but not necessarily a communist in practice. When communism becomes a philosophical problem, or even a significant dream, it is no longer vital and the people speaking of its vitality are refusing to ask the crucial questions that would make communism apparent.

The unfocused rebellions that are emerging globally do indeed prove the importance of communism by revealing the limits of the capitalist reality. However, we demonstrate a certain measure of fearfulness over the importance of these rebellions if our suggestions, when we bother to make them, result in tailing the masses—those masses whose rebellions are vague enough to be fantastical—and hoping they will magically bring communism into being. The Arab Spring, Occupy, the next uprising: why do we look to these examples as expressions of communism instead of looking to those movements, organized militantly under a communist ideology, that are making more coherent and revolutionary demands? These are movements that have not forgotten that communism is a necessity, that are not enamoured by the rediscovery of a name that only fell out of favour in the centres of global capitalism.

Those who understand communism as only an hypothesis, a horizon, a possibility are also those who are incapable of bridging the gap between theory and practice. The act of making communism a reality is generally unpleasant—but so is reality. If we have learned anything from the last two earth-shaking revolutions, it is that bringing communism into being is a messy business. Here we must re-member Mao's aphorism that revolution is not a din-ner party but a tragically violent upheaval in which one class seeks to displace another—and the ruling classes we seek to displace will not easily abdicate the historical stage.

To speak of communism as a necessity, then, is to focus on the concrete world and ask what steps are necessary to make it a reality. If the point of neces-sity is also, as Engels wagered, a scientific axiom, then perhaps it makes sense to treat the process of revolution in the manner of a science: something that is open to the future, that is still in develop-ment, while at the same time possessing moments of universalization that have been established through world historical victories.

Intellectuals at the centres of capitalism who are attempting to reclaim the name might give lip-service to Luxemburg's maxim "socialism or barbarism", but what the application of this maxim would mean in practice—that is, the question of how to make the necessity of communism a reality—is generally avoided. And so we must ask why these re-popu-larizations of communism contain no significant at-tempt to adequately theorize the steps necessary, in any particular context, for making communism.

If anything, those first world intellectuals en-gaged in repopularizing communism tend to make movementist strategies and tactics their default practice. Placing their faith in disorganized rebellions, they argue either explicitly or implicitly that we must tail every unfocused mass protest that erupts in response to global capitalism. The argument, though not always stated, is that these protests will, through some inexplicable mechanism of combination, produce a revolutionary critical mass, at some point on the distant horizon, that will finally resolve the communist hypothesis—this is precisely what is now called *movementism*.

There was a time, in the late 1990s and early 2000s, where most of us believed this movementist strategy was synonymous with revolutionary praxis. We went to Seattle to protest the World Trade Organization; we assembled in Quebec City to challenge the Free Trade Agreement of the Americas; we proclaimed that we were part of a beautiful and fragmented chaos of affinity groups, conflicted organizations, disorganized rebels, all of whom were somehow part of the same social movement that was greater than the sum of its parts. We believed ourselves to be raindrops that would produce a flood capable of sweeping away capitalism, unwilling to recognize that this was perhaps a false analogy and that we were more accurately, in very concrete terms, a disorganized mob of enraged plebeians shaking our fists at a disciplined imperial army. Years ago we spoke of "social movementism" but now it only makes sense to drop the "social" since this phase of confusion was incapable of understanding the social terrain.

So while we should endorse every rebellion against capitalism and imperialism, no matter how desperate (as Frantz Fanon once put it), we should also realize that the unfocused nature of these rebellions is intrinsically incapable of responding to the problem of necessity. As the Parti Communiste Révolutionnaire [PCR-RCP] argued in its 2006 document, *How We Intend To Fight*:

> the ruling [political] tendency… has totally assimilated the idea that there is no more unity. For them, social facts are like a bag of marbles that fall on the ground in all directions and with no common trajectory, and they want everybody to think of this as being a normal fact. […] As a matter of fact, the current situation tells us that many movements "tumble," like Mao said (or they will stumble in the following period), because they refuse to see things in their entirety. They preserve this concept of a bag of marbles and like to see multiplication of trajectories, solutions, possibilities, alternatives and reform projects. It is a rather accommodating, yet ineffective diversity.[5]

5. PCR-RCP, *How We Intend to Fight* (http://www.pcr-rcp.ca/old/pdf/pwd/3.pdf), 13.

This passage concludes, a few paragraphs later, that "[t]his path goes nowhere and will literally be punctured by the facts of the decades to come. Will we overcome this division, or will the bourgeoisie completely crush us?" It goes nowhere because, due to its very nature, it cannot approach the point of unity—the point of theoretical and practical totality that the post-modernists warned us to avoid—that should emanate from the understanding that communism is a necessity. For when we speak of necessities we also have to speak of building a unified movement that, due to this unity, will possess the intention of making what is necessary a reality. Disparate, unfocused, and divided movements lack a unified intentionality; they have proved themselves incapable of pursuing the necessity of communism.

The all-too-easy movementist solution, either implicit or explicit in these new endorsements of communism, should be understood as an assimilation of an idea of disunity that has, indeed, become "a normal fact" at the centres of capitalism. In 2003, the anti-globalization editorial collective, "Notes from Nowhere", put together a book called *We Are Everywhere* that argued:

> different movements around the world are busy strengthening their networks, developing their autonomy, taking to the streets in huge carnivals against capital, resisting brutal repression

and growing stronger as a result, and exploring new notions of sharing power rather than wielding it. Our voices are mingling in the fields and on the streets across the planet, where seemingly separate movements converge and the wave of global resistance becomes a tsunami causing turbulence thousands of miles away, and simultaneously creating ripples which lap at our doorstep.[6]

Lovely words, to be sure, but what happened to the movements this book documented—movements that were meant to converge, without taking power, in a "movement of movements"[7] and end capitalism? From movements as disparate as the EZLN in Mexico to the Ontario Coalition Against Poverty [OCAP] in Toronto, the disunified terrain in which this book placed its hope evaporated within a few years of the book's publication. For it was never really united with a focused intention dedicated to the necessary end of capitalism. Dream-like and carnivalesque, these were movements that might or might not have been important rebellions but could never produce revolution.

It is significant, perhaps, that *We Are Everywhere*

---

6. Notes from Nowhere, *We Are Everywhere* (London: Verso, 2003), 29.

7. Ibid., 511.

concludes with a poetic excerpt from Arundhati Roy's *Come September* speech: "Another world is not only possible, she is on her way. On a quiet day, I can hear her breathing." But Roy has transgressed the boundaries of movementism—today she spends a great deal of time defending the people's war in India, a revolutionary movement that would have greatly offended the editors of this book and their idealist proclamations of making revolution without taking power. Roy's shift in strategy is significant because, if read in historical context, this chronicle of the previous and failed movementist approach to revolution is an opening, an invitation, to a new return to the communist necessity it refused to address.

Another downfall of the movementist approach to revolution is that it is incapable, due to the very fact of its disorganization, of producing consistent historical memory—for how can we have such a memory if we are focused on incoherence and thus, ultimately, forgetting? As such, it is only natural that last decade's movementism would be echoed by the still popular movementism of this decade. Perhaps it makes sense that the proudly edited and published collection of today's movementism would also echo the collection of the past movementism: now we have a book called *We Are Many* that is focused on the so-called "Arab Spring" and the "Occupy Movement" and, generally amnesiatic about the fate of the movements in *We Are Everywhere*, recycles the same tropes. And it is in this general context where we find the odd intellectual speaking of communist hypotheses, possibilities, horizons—a context that remains ignorant of the preceding context which established nothing because it was incapable of accomplishing anything.

So why, then, do those who now speak of communism desire a continuation of this ineffective practice that, at least in the period documented by the "Notes from Nowhere" collective, was wary of uttering this banned name? To go further than simply speak the name is an act of fear and trembling, a terrified remembering of a past experience that we have been told was cataclysmic.

Here, at the centres of capitalism, we have inherited a suspicion of a project we have been socialized into believing was nothing more than totalitarianism, a brutal "Animal Farm" that can teach us nothing. So when only the name, and not the necessity behind the name, is reclaimed, this deficient way of seeing the world is inherited. And from this inheritance, because we do not want to conceptualize a return that will both continue and rupture from these past revolutions, the only praxis we can imagine is another articulation of the same movementism that, once upon a time, was even suspicious of communism.

For it is a fearful thing to direct oneself towards actually making communism. Talk is cheap in the face of necessity; talk that avoids necessity will only lead to failure because, refusing to conceptualize praxis as something more than a philosophical problem (and in this refusal remobilizing the same movementist categories), we will remain trapped on the abstract level of appearance rather than descending to the concrete realm of necessity:

> By only sticking to the appearance and subjectivity born out of any given situation, by remaining blind to the totality of the movement in denying the links and mediations, we give rise to a practice which moves far from the true power of the struggle. It is a waste; it is as if we refuse the immense and superb capabilities of the revolutionary struggle. The petty-bourgeoisie may be able to ignore and go without this potential but the proletariat cannot. [...] That is why we say that in the current situation... nothing is more right, useful and constructive than to struggle for developing a genuine and 'common class' project. Therefore, we mean to conceive our tools, our methods and our objectives under the terms and conditions of totality and unity. We have a great need for conceiving this revolutionary struggle. We must carry out 'the interests of the movement as a whole.'[8]

---

8. PCR-RCP, *How We Intend to Fight*, 14.

And carrying out the interests of the movement as a whole, a demand produced by the intentionality of necessity, is something no errant hypothesis and no imagined horizon, still land-locked within the movementist terrain, can produce.

science and necessity

Before examining the phenomenon of movementism in more detail, however, it is worth pausing to think about the word *science* that, from its very first utterance, places us beyond the pale of polite activist discourse. We now live in a time where this word is treated as suspect by many involved in anti-capitalist projects; woe betide those who would connect it to the word *revolutionary* and speak of a scientific assessment of struggle!

There are, of course, laudable reasons behind this suspicion. We know how the scientific method and scientific labour have been used by capitalism. We understand the horrors of technologies adapted to military logic, of the vicious and exclusionary nature of the medical-industrial complex, of the sciences harnessed by colonial and imperial projects to categorize, control, and dehumanize subject populations, of the ways in which science has acted as a discourse to promote the interests of the ruling classes. We rightly mock the "scientific" gibberish of evolutionary psychology and other bio-determinist nonsense. Decades of critical theory and philosophy has made us cynical.

But what has this totalizing cynicism produced? On the one hand, a scornful mistrust of the word science when it is used to speak of history and social change on the part of those who benefit, by living at the centres of global capitalism, from a monopoly of scientific advancement. On the other hand, a conscious anti-scientism and flight back into mysticism that was not only evident in the US hippy movement of the 1960s, but in every contemporary collaboration with religious obscurantism.

Both rejections of science combine and diverge in every movementist space. Often we encounter a suspicion of science premised on the assumption that it is a European dogma, not different from a religion, that suppresses the world-views of those who were Europe's victims. While we should be aware that colonial conquest was, in part, achieved through a cultural suppression where the spirituality of the colonizer (i.e. Judeo-Christianity) was treated as "rational" (and perhaps even, though wrongly, *scientific*) in comparison to the supposed "barbaric" spirituality of the colonized, there is a problem with "europeanizing" science as a whole. Here, science is treated as a colonial practice and spirituality the business of the colonized; the latter may even be fetishized and, in this fetishism, appropriated in the most racist, though implicit, sense of the term. Assuming that science is something "invented" by Europeans, however, is to erase all of the scientific practices and discoveries of those peoples European colonialism genocided and colonized, stealing and claiming scientific discoveries in the process.

If we are to reclaim the immediacy of communism-as-necessity then we must also reclaim the conceptual meaning of science. In the crudest sense of scientific advancement—of technological instruments—this fact should be obvious. Capitalism possesses a monopoly over those technologies that are capable of maintaining social control: guns, tanks, drones, etc. We will not topple this brutal system through meditation of any sort, let alone our moral and spontaneous will to "speak truth to power" in innumerable demonstrations where the state's police and military are better prepared than the average protestor. Movementism has already produced a mythology of struggle that would lead us to believe otherwise, a moralism that runs counter to reality—wishful thinking that if we are all out in the streets, all spontaneously producing an insurrection, the state's technological machines will refuse to initiate a blood bath.

Let us go deeper into this problem, though, so as to think the possibility of scientific thought. To reclaim the concept of science is more than simply recognizing the efficacy of instruments; it concerns anti-capitalist theory itself. And to argue that there is such a thing as a *revolutionary science* is even bolder than arguing for the necessary recognition of the scientific instruments monopolized by the ruling classes. Here is a totalizing assumption: science should find its home at the heart of theories of organization and strategy because science, the only thing capable of generating facts and truths, is superior to non-science.

What do we mean, then, by science? In the previous section I briefly discussed how science is open to the future, a process in development that produces, through historical struggle, universal truths (that is, facts that are applicable in every particular context, though also mediated by these contexts). Although science is often defined in popular discourse as the empirical method utilized by those disciplines that we are educated to understand as "properly" scientific, such a definition is about as useful as saying "biology is biology" or "chemistry is chemistry" and ignores the logical basis that makes these disciplines different from non-scientific theoretical terrains. The empirical method is indeed important, and is a significant tool for establishing truths in particular scientific disciplines, but to reduce the definition of science to "empiricism" results in positivism—which is precisely what many of us have learned to suspect whenever the word *science* is spoken.

Science is that which speaks to material conditions without mystification; science provides a natural explanation of natural phenomena. Physics is a physical explanation of physical phenomena; biology is a biological explanation of biological phenomena; chemistry is a chemical explanation of chemical phenomena; and historical materialism is an historical/social explanation of historical/social phenomena. Why, then, is historical materialism a *revolutionary science*? Because the historical/social explanation of historical/social phenomena is the very mechanism of class struggle, of revolution. And this scientific hypothesis is that which is capable of demystifying the whole of history and myriad societies, a way in which to gauge any and every social struggle capable of producing historical change.

Hence, without a scientific understanding of social struggle we are incapable of recognizing when and where failed theories manifest. The physicist has no problem banning Newtonian speculation to the past where it belongs; s/he possesses a method of assessment based on the development of a specific scientific terrain. If we resist a similar scientific engagement with social struggle we have no method of making sense of the ways in which revolutionary hypotheses have been disproven in the historical crucible due to historical "experiments" of class struggle.

To reject a scientific understanding of struggle is to assert that these past experiments—the complete failures, the half-successes, the half-failures—have failed to establish anything significant, and so we are doomed to successive attempts at directionless reinvention.

A scientific understanding of struggle, however, teaches us about the theoretical terrain of struggle that has been presented by history, through humanity's past endeavours, and is still open to the future. Which social struggles established new truths due to marginal, but universalizable successes? Which successive social struggles learned from these past establishments of truth and went a little further before also meeting failure? How, then, do we apply what has been scientifically proven in these social experiments to our particular circumstances so as to go even further? These are questions that can only be asked if we have the meter of science to gauge our practice thus demanding, at every moment of struggle, an attention to necessity. Without such an understanding of reality, we have no way of making sense of our practice; we might as well forget the past, act as if everything is particularly unique, and ignore every moment when the repetition of failure ought to be treated as obvious.

Movementism receives its strength in this grand project of forgetting.

puritanism

The puritan pilgrims who led the colonization of North America believed that they stood in opposition to the dogmatism of mainstream Christianity; they refused to recognize a similar dogmatism in their rigid morality, in their hatred of the Church of England and the Papists of Rome. Since movementism finds its theoretical centre in the most powerful nations of the Western Hemisphere, despite being echoed and encouraged by similar tendencies in Europe, perhaps it is only natural that this sense of puritan self-righteousness—this Protestant ethic of decentralization and disunified theoretical praxis—would eventually hamper the social movements in the US and Canada.

It would be rather simplistic, however, to reduce the current cult of disorganized activism to a sentiment inherited from the predominant religious ideology of these nations' establishment. Such an analogy, however, is only interesting as an exercise in hermeneutics; it is better to simply accept that a dogmatic commitment to a supposed non-dogmatism exists rather than speculate on its possibly arcane ideological origins. There are other factors, after all, some of which may provide greater explanatory depth and many that intersect and combine: generations of anti-communism, the collapse of actually existing socialism, the comparative level of privilege enjoyed by those who live at the centres of capitalism.

If anything, the analogy of puritan Protestantism might be able to explain the self-righteous need to arrogantly cling to the movementist strategy in the face of historical evidence. Better to accept only the evidence of actually existing socialism's failures, its supposed totalitarianism, just as the fundamentalist accepts only the evidence that the world is irrevocably fallen and writhing in sin. In this sense, the movementist horizon becomes akin to the rapture.

This desire to cling to decentralized activist organizing is evident in the constant appeal to methods, politics, and scattered social movements that were enshrined by the past movementist cycle. The lingering fascination with the EZLN, for example, is telling: there is a reason that the Zapatistas have received sainthood while the Sendero Luminoso has not. The latter's aborted people's war placed it firmly in the realm of failure; the former, in refusing to attempt a seizure of state power, were to escape any resemblance of a catastrophic communism. But when a movement actually tries to take power, and goes so far as to almost succeed, in its collapse the meaning of its actions will be written by the ruling class intelligentsia and everyone beholden to the common sense of this class. Organizations such as the EZLN have avoided the fate of the PCP because they did not walk the same path of revolutionary necessity that is often tragic and brutal—where there will always be mistakes, where the problem of differing class morality produces ethical confusion, where failure is more spectacular with each heightened level of struggle.[9]

Maybe the desire to cling to movementism speaks more to a desire for a political purity free from the taint of necessity. Beneath this desire for purity, then, a fear of necessity: we do not want to confront what it would mean to address the dilemma of *socialism or barbarism* because the only movements we endorse are those that have never developed far enough to treat this question as anything more than

---

9. None of this is to say, however, that the experience of the EZLN should be dismissed or that this organization will remain in revolutionary limbo. They still exist and, like any movement that is able to persist, are not necessarily static in their theory and practice. Here, I am more interested in the over-fetishization of the politics they expressed in the 1990s, with the emphasis on refusing to take power, and the way they were conceptualized by USAmericans and Canadians who were looking for a movement to express their eclectic politics—hence the reason more than one academic called the EZLN's movement "the first postmodern revolution". But at the same time, just as we should reject the eurocentric fetishization of the Zapatistas, we should also reject the eurocentric rejection based on fidelity to some ortho-Trotskyist notion of class struggle. For more detail on this latter problem, the reader should consider Bromma's *Racist "Anti-Imperialism"? Class, Colonialism and the Zapatistas* (http://kersplebedeb.com/posts/racist-anti-imperialism).

an abstraction.

But this was always the problem with move-mentism, a symptom of the past cycle of disorganized struggle where everything communist was rejected a priori as a dead end. At the very least we can understand this previous rejection as a product of the times: actually existing socialism had only crumbled a decade earlier, the ruling class ideologues were working overtime to foster the belief that communism was irrelevant, and most activists living at the centres of imperialism (typically myopic when it comes to most of the world) were largely ignorant of the new round of communist struggle that was erupting in the global peripheries. Even the fact that the anti-globalization anarchists were capable of noticing an armed movement outside of the first world was surprising—though the reason they would choose to focus on the Zapatistas instead of the Senderistas was perhaps predictable. Still, at least that stage of movementism was a sign of the times, the product of a defeated working class movement in the world's most privileged nations.

The past cycle of movementist struggle declared fragmentation and disunification to be virtuous in an attempt to distance itself from fallen communism. But now we have a strange hybrid: a reclamation of communism as an abstraction that asserts itself in the midst of renewed movementism that is no different in practice from the movementism that dismissed communism as a dead-end. Thus, all these attempts to reclaim communism cannot help but sublimate the sentiments of anti-communist movementism. The only difference is in the jargon, in an abstract desire to save a terminology rather than a concrete practice.

And yet the truth is that this abstract reclamation of communism has come too late. The movementism of today shares the same problems as the movementism of yesterday regardless of the reclamation of communism on the part of some. Thus we find movements that are still built upon nebulous theoretical foundations, composed predominantly of people who might not be interested in even communism's name, and ideologues attempting to speak for these movements in a manner that might be perceived as alien.

These movements often emerge from popular rebellions and those who attempt to explain their disunification will appeal to common slogans and concepts. The ideologues of the past cycle of movementism were at least humble enough to recognize this element of disarticulation; they were also theoretically consistent when they treated this disarticulation as a virtue but refused to call it communism. Today's grey eminences, in their desire to reestablish the name communism as simply an abstract notion, are trying to brand a series of disorganized and limited rebellions according to their own conceptual constellation. Hence the problem of tailism where the attempt to popularize the name communism amounts to running behind a rebellion that rejects articulation, attempting to make it conform to a jargon that it would otherwise reject because the fact of its disorganization makes it allergic to theoretical and practical unity.

Even worse is the fact that those who are attempting to reclaim communism end up catching the same plague that infects the movements they tail: the fear of necessity. It is one thing for an activist involved in the Occupy movement to reject all of the principles of past communisms, to dismiss world historical revolutions; it is quite another thing for those who want to renew the tradition of communism to act in the same manner and, in the midst of this performance, worry about alienating themselves by speaking of a concrete communism.

Better to just tail the masses, without even wondering at the class composition of the masses that are being tailed. Better to hope that this rebellion is a revolutionary movement, and that we can influence its direction with our books about "hypotheses" and "horizons" instead of wondering about the problems of strategy and historical efficacy. We must wonder when the now mostly defunct *Occupied Wallstreet Journal* refuses to communicate anything openly communist and yet is being edited by known communists: in the manic flurry to become part of this current round of rebellions we have inherited the movementist fear of necessity. And in this context it is no wonder that we are terrified of speaking anything but the name of communism.

sectarianism

The shibboleth of *sectarianism* is one of the common excuses for endorsing the most banal forms of movementist praxis. After all, if a unified revolutionary movement requires, by its very definition, a unified theory, then such a theory necessarily excludes other theoretical approaches. While it is true that every theoretically unified organization will experience multiple and competing *political* lines, it is also true that there cannot be a unified movement in which contradictory *theoretical* lines operate; the fantasy of movementism is that there can indeed be this type of multiplicity that, despite this fragmentation, will spontaneously produce an apocalyptic moment of unity.

Hence, any talk of the necessity of a revolutionary organization unified in and disciplined by a coherent theory must be judged as heretical by movementism's ideologues and adherents. To speak of this necessity is to be charged with pushing an exclusionary political line, fostering "division", and behaving in a sectarian manner. Amongst those committed to movementism, then, it is a great sin to reject this approach and argue instead for a praxis in which revolutions have been made historically: the sectarians, here, are similar to the heretics of the Catholic Church who were excommunicated for promoting rebel sects.

Clearly, we would be remiss if we were to argue that sectarianism is not a problem. We know that there are some marxists and marxist organizations, most of whom act as if they are still living in the first two decades of the 20th century, that are indeed frightfully sectarian. These tiny grouplets are incapable of participating in coalitions, dogmatically unwilling to engage in meaningful ideological line struggle, and spend most of their energy attacking other small sects that are similar to themselves. Their political praxis is little more than an act of religious self-righteousness where they imagine themselves to be the guardians of a pure marxist theory that must be protected from historical contamination.

But the charge of sectarianism is levelled at every and any organization that dares to question the fundamental movementist doctrine. The charge of sectarianism is also meant to imply that the "sectarians" are dogmatists, and in some cases this is indeed correct. But the very fact that they are being charged with sectarianism—because they are refusing to abide by what is intended to be a hegemonic doctrine—is due to their unwillingness to declare fidelity to movementism. They are sectarian simply because they are seen as *sects* who have broken from what those who are making the charge deem the normative terrain of anti-capitalism. Thus, the very charge of sectarianism is often generated by a dogmatic unwillingness to question social movementism.

In this charge there is also a myth: that people or organizations united around particular revolutionary principles are responsible for the worst excesses of the left in the 20th century. Made by people who have rarely bothered to think through revolutionary history, this is a charge that is levelled at any ideology that possesses principled clarity. Essentially, the charge is unprincipled; those making it would prefer a lack of principles, a willingness to unite behind any vague standard, a rejection of theoretical struggle. Here we discover an intentional amnesia regarding what was actually significant in anti-capitalist history: anti-revisionist movements that, in their principled refusal to peacefully co-exist with capitalism, launched innumerable revolutions—some of which were world historical.

Beyond this very crude and etymological understanding of sectarianism, however, where we can understand the word (sectarian) by its root (sect), we need to go further and examine the concept of the word that is obscured by the name. For sectarianism means something more than the theory and practice of a sect, just as the word *hegemony* means something more than the polity of a *hegemon*. And the way in which the charge of sectarianism is commonly used by the normative movementist left demonstrates a failure to understand the word's conceptual depth.

A dyed-in-the-wool sectarian is someone who declares complete fidelity to the principle of political difference and, in this declaration, accepts this principle as their primary operating ideology. The sectarian will not engage with people outside of their sect, except to treat them as enemies, because they fear ideological pollution. The sectarian closes their self from history, treats their ideology as sacrosanct, and advocates cultish behaviour. The sectarian imagines that their sect possesses a completed truth and, due to this great act of imagining, refuses to recognize that the lack of growth in this sect is a sign of stagnation. An organization that is sectarian will not grow in any significant manner, and will remain doomed to political irrelevance, due to a rigid dogmatism that can only collect those adherents that every religious cult preys upon: a small minority of religious-minded individuals who are looking for easy answers, desire an excuse to act in a self-righteous manner, and are generally maladjusted troglodytes who dream of leading the masses even as they despise these masses for failing to recognize the great truths of their sect.

But principled political difference by itself does not amount to sectarianism, though it is often treated as such by those who would judge any moment of principled difference as sectarian heresy. Indeed, if endorsing a principled and politically different revolutionary ideology was the measure of sectarianism, then Marx and Engels would have to be sectarian for daring to wage an ideological line struggle against the other and utopian socialist approaches that threatened to mislead the movement in the 19th century. Let us go further so as to understand how this definition is completely absurd: if we were to define the concept of sectarianism as simply "principled political difference" then we would have to also accept that all anti-capitalists, even movementists, are sectarian insofar as they maintain a principled political difference with pro-capitalists.

Maintaining a principled political difference is itself a necessity, part of developing a movement capable of drawing demarcating lines, and even those who would endorse movementism have to do so if they are to also maintain their anti-capitalism. Political lines can and must be drawn: the enemy draws them, and thus understands that we are the enemy, and so we need to have the very same understanding if we are to survive. Only liberals, who imagine that there really is no enemy and that everyone will get along under the peace of welfare capitalism, believe that the drawing of these lines is a violent act that—like violence itself—is immoral because it is the way in which the enemy behaves. In this context, however, the liberal stands within the lines drawn by this enemy and is thus incapable of understanding that they are endorsing a reality determined by the most insidious and immanent violence.

Moreover, political differences do matter because there are significant differences between political ideologies. The praxis of movementism, despite some of its adherents' claims about big tent socialism, is generally based on an anarchist assessment of reality and is thus, in itself, a political ideology at odds with those its adherents would seek to pull into its orbit. Disparate marxist approaches are indeed quite different in how they understand the political fault-lines and what needs to be done. To pretend that all of these trajectories are ultimately the same—metaphorically similar workers with identical tools attacking the identical problem[10]— is a myth fostered by those who imagine that class

10. This analogy is drawn from a comic by Stephanie McMillan (http://stephaniemcmillan.org/2013/04/23/ sectarianism/) where she makes the same banal point about sectarianism, conflating the word sectarian with the concept of political difference.

struggle is homogeneous despite their claims about the importance of heterogeneity. Movementism demands a homogeneity that masquerades as heterogeneity: a multiplicity of trajectories but if and only if these trajectories recognize that the overall approach is correct and do not dare to organize outside of the movementist praxis or call it into question.

The maoist is not identical to the trotskyist; the marxist is not identical to the anarchist: their tools are not the same, their grasp of the object with which they are engaging is not precisely identical. To pretend otherwise is about as useful as pretending that Marx and Engels were the same as Proudhon and Duhring, forgetting the ideological war waged against these differences so as to define the terrain of revolutionary theory.

Some of those who speak now of communist hypotheses and horizons, who are attempting to revise the word without critical attention to its concrete historical development as a revolutionary concept, are the same people who would have us believe that these theoretical differences do not matter. Thus, the dismal charge of sectarianism is yet another example of the fear of necessity. Ideological line struggles are indeed necessary.

We must not forget that part of the communist necessity is to draw political lines of demarcation and to understand, in this moment of drawing, the forces of revolution and counter-revolution. And a further line must be drawn between those who would treat communism as a necessity—and in this treatment learn from the past world historical revolutions—and those who would treat it only as a hypothesis, a horizon, an ideal possibility.

chapter two:
collaboration & contingency

Despite the unwillingness to examine the riddle of necessity, to speak directly to its demands, there is often the a priori recognition of its fact. All of these nebulous attempts to reassert communism must accept, even in their inability to make concrete assessments, that the end of capitalism is necessary—though not, it must be admitted and accepted, preordained. Some attempts go so far as to summon the name of Lenin and other revolutionaries. Jodi Dean, for example, speaks of the need for a leninist style of organization, a significant and laudable statement on the part of a popular academic. Unfortunately, her leninism is reduced to a form without content—a better organized Occupy, something that emerges spontaneously from Occupy.

There are times when she claims that communism cannot be deferred indefinitely, but with such a defanged leninism, that will invent processes as it spontaneously develops, the revolution can only be deferred; her horizon remains distant.[11]

So after all this talk of horizons and ideal forms, necessity itself is recognized only insofar as it hovers as a storm over that distant horizon. After denouncing the usual aspects of the communist past according to a vague "anti-Stalinist" narrative, to conjure the name of Lenin is like a stage trick. After speaking of revolutionary processes that will emerge spontaneously through struggle, it is strange to argue against deferring communism indefinitely—which is precisely what the practice she valorizes presumes.

It is difficult to know what we should make of this recognition of necessity, sometimes sublimated and sometimes reified. For if the concept of necessity is an assumption pushed under this new discourse of communism, or an abstract notion perceived as an ideal form, then it ceases to matter. The questions it demands, the historical experiences it has produced, are left either misconceived or unanswered.

Pushing the concept of necessity to the margins, the politics mobilized (or, rather, under-mobilized)

_____

11. Jodi Dean, *The Communist Horizon* (London: Verso, 2012), 207-250.

by this discourse generates the appearance of radicalism unmoored from concrete foundations. Hence the proliferation of various groups promoting an exciting new radicalism free from our supposedly boring revolutionary past: the Invisible Committee and its "coming insurrection"; the prior Tiqqun group and its nebulous notion of "bloom"; Franco Berardi's linguistic revolution that explicitly denies historical necessity. Theory wrenched from the framework of revolutionary science can only be radical in form. Perhaps this was always the intent: fear either supervenes—fear of the necessities demanded by an actual revolutionary movement—or is sublimated, beneath the appearance of radicalism, along with the concept of necessity itself.

In this context, then, we must ask why the unfolding theory, hard-won through world historical revolution, is considered obtuse and alienating by the same people who never tire of inventing "new" and impenetrable concepts, whose writing seems intentionally opaque, and whose radicalism appears to be little more than an intellectual exercise. What should those of us who declare fidelity to a revolutionary communism that emerged from the experience of class struggle care for a theory that primarily locates its radicalism on the level of appearance—that is obscure and abstract, that properly belongs at an academic conference rather than in the streets and countryside? For these theoretical abstractions are indeed only popular amongst first world academics and dilettantes, students and would-be intellectuals, anarchists from middle-class suburbs searching for words and ideas to guarantee a revolutionary ideology. At the margins and in the peripheries these theories have gained very little credence.

These contemporary manifestos, greeted with excitement by a small population of radicals at the centres of capitalism, are not as new as their champions believe. The working-class movement, the revolutionary struggle of the masses, has experienced innumerable and similar attempts to revise revolutionary theory. Eugen Duhring, for example, attempted to provide an alternative and prettier theory to the supposed boringness of communist ideology, and though the theoretical categories he used might now seem hackneyed, this is only because we have the privilege of historical perspective. Duhring was, in fact, drawing upon a conceptual constellation that a late nineteenth century intellectual would have understood and found exciting, a constellation that had little to do with the concrete experience of the European proletariat of that period. Duhring's influence was significant enough amongst intellectuals flirting with socialism that other prominent thinkers treated him as an equally prominent representative of socialism: Nietzsche's various and confused attacks on socialism come mainly from his reading of Duhring (there is no evidence that Nietzsche ever read Marx or Engels); Herzl's Zionism, along with the Dreyfus affair, was partially influenced by an assumption that socialism was anti-semitic due to an understanding of socialism derived from Duhring who was also an anti-semite.[12] But now we only know Duhring because Engels took the time to thoroughly destroy his theoretical doctrine and, in doing so, prove the strength of what Duhring took to be out-of-step with intellectual fashion.

To Duhring we can add Guy Debord and Situationism, a theory that crystallized during the Paris rebellion of 1968 and that is still beloved by those activists obsessed with vague theoretical-praxis such as culture jamming, psycho-geography, and other abstract concepts that are compelling because

---

12. The fact that these conservative thinkers, whose philosophies have been associated with every form of political reaction, focused on Duhring's socialism rather than the revolutionary currents represented by Marx and Engels is worth some reflection. Perhaps when socialist intellectuals make a big deal about a specific thinker their anti-socialist counterparts—the ideologues of the ruling class—follow the lead of the former and mistake chic radicalism as more significant than it actually is. Glenn Beck, for example, has done more to popularize *The Coming Insurrection* than the Invisible Committee itself. Of course, the Invisible Committee, unlike Duhring, is not anti-semitic, and Beck, unlike Nietzsche, is an intellectual troll.

of their obscurantism. And though Debord might have had no significant impact on concrete struggle even in the context from which he emerged (it might even be accurate to claim that Situationism matters little to even most academic leftists these days) he is worth mentioning because so many of these "new" attempts at reclaiming communism often speak his name.

There are other names and other attempts, and those that were not preserved by academic and publishing institutions were forgotten by the end of the 1980s when the communism they sought to revise was supposedly defeated. More than a critical reflection of supposedly "orthodox" communism, these eclectic or overly academic communisms are the symptom of a larger problem: the inability to overcome normative ideology even in the midst of recognizing its existence.

At the centres of capitalism, where capitalist hegemony is generally complete, we have been trained since birth to accept the ruling ideas of the ruling class as common sense. Although we have been successful in stepping outside of this common sense in order to recognize the need to end capitalism, we are often incapable of apprehending the meaning of this necessity due to how we have been taught to perceive the world. We have been taught failure, we have been educated to believe precisely what a class ideology that is concerned with preserving the current state of affairs claims about the history of class struggle. So when we step outside of the end of history narrative it is easier to gravitate towards those supposedly critical strains of communism, dismiss what these strains name as "orthodoxy" according to the standard of capitalist propaganda, and embrace "new" communist ventures.

This is what the Invisible Committee is and what its predecessor, the Tiqqun group, was; this is Berardi's *Uprising*, unintentionally satirical with its imaginary revolution; this is what all of these similar reclamations of communism, from Endnotes to Théorie Communiste, are and can ever be: an attempt to profess communism while simultaneously accepting the end of history narrative. This is why the vast majority of these supposed reclamations of communism refuse to speak of the vital revolutionary struggles that have emerged at the peripheries of global imperialism; this is why there is rarely any mention of people's wars.

In such a context the only solution is to tail popular rebellions and, in this tailing, refuse to provide active and unified leadership. The theoretical constellation might differ but the practice remains the same: movementism, with its presumption that the disorganization of social movements is an unqualified virtue. To intervene in these spaces and attempt to provide leadership is treated as an act of violence; if an organization of the leninist style is indeed needed, then we are led to believe that it must invent itself overnight, spontaneously emerging from the next rebellion.

But in this context there are several questions worth asking. Why are there so many new manifestos aimed at delinking from the communist past, and what do they accomplish? Why do academics have an obsession with an opaque theory that resonates primarily with these same academics and activist intellectuals? What theoretical constellation is being dismissed as old-fashioned, boring, and orthodox? And just what does it mean to reclaim the concept of necessity as something that is neither sublimated nor reified? Again, it is worth pointing out that these are questions that are mainly pertinent at the centres of capitalism where we lost our way a long time ago. So we also need to ask the most important question that haunts all of these questions, which is a question of necessity: how do we find our way back to the road of communist revolution? For the moment, however, let us put aside this last question to focus on the haunting itself.

the haunted past

So what should we make of every new manifesto that attempts to delink communism from its revolutionary past? At the very least we should begin by recognizing that many of these reassertions of communism are not total rejections of history; significant names and movements are occasionally noted, and this is a partial victory. Dean conjures the ghost of Lenin, Badiou appeals to the spectre of Mao. The gap between name and concept is occasionally bridged; sometimes there is a recognition that certain elements of history are ours to reclaim. Badiou, who once defined himself as a Maoist against intellectual fashion, remains unwilling to surrender historical memory to capitalist ideology—he goes so far as to challenge the discourse of "totalitarianism" that identifies Stalin with Hitler.[13] In some of these cases, then, there is a laudable attempt, and an ideological struggle, to return a variety of names to what is considered acceptable discourse even amongst left-wing academia. In 2007 Slavoj Zizek, Sebastian Budgen, and Stathis Kouvelakis initiated the opening salvo of this reclamation by releasing the collection *Lenin Reloaded*, an attempt to make

---

13. Alain Badiou, *The Communist Hypothesis* (London: Verso, 2010), 3.

Lenin palatable for academics and intellectuals at the centres of capitalism.

Before this reassertion of communism as a name, and under the auspices of a simplified marxism or socialism, it was inappropriate to speak of Lenin—let alone Mao or Stalin—unless we were speaking of the "betrayal" of some vague socialist ideal. Indeed, those trotskyists and post-trotskyists who were the primary authorities of marxism in first world academia would only speak of Lenin outside of an academic setting. They were obviously content to accept the discourse that compared Stalin to Hitler, due to their obsession with an imaginary stalinism, just as they were happy to ban the name of Mao from acceptable discourse. Thus, we should at least recognize the significance of this reclamation.

And yet the rearticulation of communism, regardless of the names that are often mobilized, still persists in the delinking of communism from its revolutionary past. Although such a delinking appears to be laudable, these manifestos resonate with those raised in the so-called "end of history" where anti-communist ideology is ascendant. Moreover, many of these reclamations still refuse to speak those banned names since they remained convinced of their betrayal. All attempts to alienate ourselves from our revolutionary history can be presented as pragmatic and critical.

The desire to close those historical doors through

which the ghosts of past revolutions emerge has been the tactical practice of radical anti-capitalists at the centres of global capitalism for a long time, crystallizing after the collapse of actually existing socialism. Even before this collapse it was often the hallmark of supposedly "critical" marxism in the first world, perhaps due to the influence of trotsky-ism, to denounce every real world socialism as stalin-ist, authoritarian, totalitarian. Since the reification of anti-communist triumphalism this denunciation has achieved hegemony; it is the position to which would-be marxist academics gravitate and accept as common sense, an unquestioned dogma. Hence, we are presented with a constellation of attempts to re-boot communism by calling it something different, by making its past either taboo or meaningless, by resorting to a self-defeating philosophy where the idea of a "true" communism is eternally conjured in order to dismiss past revolutions due to their inabil-ity to demonstrate fidelity to this pure idea.

Beneath these attempts to alienate communism from its past we occasionally discover moments of Platonic idealism. Out there, somewhere, is the idea of *True Communism* upon which we must re-flect in order to reach that distant horizon of human freedom.

But the ghosts of history cannot be exorcized; at-tempting to ignore them by choosing to speak of a communism without reference to these shades will remain haunted. Most often such a discourse will presuppose, as a default principle, that this haunting means precisely what the anti-communist discourse claims it means. Occasionally it will seek a different past, skipping over the entire history of revolutionary communist experience, and pretend that utopian theories and movements—alienated, mystified, idealist—are the only worthwhile precedent for communism.

In the end, the attempt to delink from our revolutionary past, treating it as a prison from which we must escape, does violence to history. To claim that we must unshackle ourselves from this past and seek a new communist horizon is to denounce everything for which revolutionaries have fought and died. These ghosts can teach us something, both in their successes and failures, and we learn nothing by dismissing them as unwelcome poltergeists.

And yet the obsession to discover a new approach to communism that is somehow free from the past—as if we can ever escape this past that weighs upon us "like a nightmare"—prides itself in its supposed creativity and critical depth. We must ask, however, what is creative about trying to reboot a tradition by deleting its world historical moments? This is much like the cliche of reinventing the wheel: it might indeed be creative to make a triangular or octagon wheel but it is not a very meaningful creativity. And just what, precisely, is critical about building a communism by repeating the common sense anti-communist ideology about past socialisms? It is very easy to believe we are being critical by challenging the supposed dogmas of communism when, in point of fact, we are simply repeating what every capitalist textbook has been claiming about communism for decades.

The creativity and criticism of academic theory has always been rather banal. The jargon might seem exciting, the supposed newness of neologisms and clever frameworks might indeed be challenging, but there really hasn't been anything thoroughly creative and critical that has emerged from the ranks of academic speculation for a long time. There are innumerable *obscurantisme terroristes* (to cite the term Foucault once applied to Derrida), clever theorists who achieved the illusion of critical creativity by a framework defined by obscurantist jargon, but nothing that has provided a new concrete analysis of a concrete situation—nothing capable of changing the world. The exciting theory, the creative theory, the theory capable of thoroughly critiquing the world has only ever emerged from revolutionary movements. But since this was an insight of Marx and the tradition of marxism, it is only natural that non- or anti-marxist academics would dismiss this axiom and lose themselves in an obsession to produce new theories and new manifestos. None of which will ever matter to the masses, which is to say will ever be capable of doing what this kind of manifesto claims it can do in the first place—change the course of history.

Thus, we should have little patience for those who complain about the supposed poverty of thought amongst the ranks of today's anti-revisionist communisms. This constant complaining about the so-called "dogmatic" fidelity to figures such as Mao or Lenin or even Stalin—this fear and trembling caused by those who even dare to uphold the failed people's war in Peru—is a symptom of a falsely critical creativity. It is a bit like telling physicists that they are not critical or creative for daring to take the General Theory of Relativity seriously, thus proposing that it would be better just to pretend that Einstein and all of the trouble his theory caused did not exist. Most importantly, such a complaint demonstrates a very uncreative and uncritical fidelity to anti-communist ideology. We really must ask: what is so critical about accepting the fixed interpretation of the world that we've been socialized into accepting since birth? It is rather asinine to complain about dogmatism and orthodoxy if one adheres to the height of dogmatic orthodoxy: the bourgeois way of seeing the world.

Embracing the risk of sounding academically unfashionable, I want to suggest that there can be no creative or critical manifesto that exists outside the bounds of a concrete and revolutionary understanding of necessity. Specifically, and in this context, the only worthwhile manifestos are those that are capable of producing an understanding of reality as seen from *below*:

> When seen from below or seen from above, the same reality is often viewed very differently. Two different points of view, which generate two different understandings, and consequently, two different kinds of feelings and reactions... The first revolutionary act in class struggle is to recognize, understand and seize the world from below! We must not fall into the trap that is believing that the bourgeoisie's hallucinations from above are truthful reality. [...] The current world situation is a good example of this double-standard, this two-faced way of seeing things. Seen from above, everything is prosperity, enrichment, wealth and democracy. Seen from below, it is crisis, corruption, war and misery.[14]

None of these new academic manifestos, even when they veil themselves as marxist, are capable of representing the world from below. They are always above, filtering down from the heights of academic speculation, divorced from revolutionary

---

14. PCR-RCP, *How We Intend to Fight*, 5.

struggle. Concerned with a distant horizon, and not the brutal necessity that demands revolution, they are constantly looking towards a future that is unchained from the past. Here we must recall Walter Benjamin's warning in *Theses on the Philosophy of History* (for though he was also an estranged academic, he was aware of the danger of a movement premised solely on a future unshackled from its past) where he claims that this focus on a utopian horizon results in the passing of "[t]he true picture of the past" and that "every image of the past that is not recognized by the present as one of its own concerns threatens to disappear irretrievably."[15]

All this talk of new horizons must be abandoned if we cannot honestly engage with the image of our past and how it affects the present. Those horizons that are alienated from the world of below, that do not emerge as goals produced by the past struggles of the wretched of the earth, should be treated as idle speculation.

---

15. Walter Benjamin, *Illuminations* (Schocken Books: New York, 1968), 255.

contingencies

If it is unfashionable to return to the concept of *necessity* as the basis for human emancipation, it is because a theoretical tradition that forbade this concept, and instead demanded that we speak only of *contingency*, is still prevalent. This tradition, however, is prevalent primarily at the heart of first world academia and has little to do with the world-as-seen-from-below. When placed in contact with the global masses, the wretched of the earth, such a theoretical tradition might be meaningless, though it is indeed meaningful in the context of this treatise because we have been discussing, from the outset, the problem of these new manifestos with their endless talk of horizons and hypotheses—manifestos embedded in first world academia.

This embeddedness means that, regardless of any attempt to reclaim the "totalizing narrative" of communism, we are still forced to deal with all of those theoretical critiques that forbade us from speaking of the *necessity* of communism. For to speak of necessity is to deny the claim that history might be nothing more than contingent moments incapable of telling us anything significant—and that to demand necessity from this chain of contingency might be tantamount to totalitarianism.

In "Nietzsche, Genealogy and History" Michel

Foucault argued that history should be seen as nothing more than a procession of contingency, where no moment produces the necessary demand for another, and every historical development must be recognized as murderous. To speak of the necessity of revolution in this context is to also speak of a totalizing discourse, another game of power and knowledge, that is no more or less valuable than the past and future avalanches of murder which amount to history. Beyond the eternal manifestation of power-knowledge, then, there is no such thing as historical development; to imagine progress, even in the qualified sense of successive modes of production, is to subordinate the contingent and ultimately unchanging reality of history to a totalizing narrative.

Such an understanding of history can only treat revolutionary moments as further examples of murderous totalization; a revolution is no better than what it is revolting against—ultimately contingent, its claims regarding necessity little more than excuses for the exercise and mobilization of power. According to this interpretation, then, the moment of revolution is simply another meaningless cipher in a swamp of contingent expressions of power-knowledge. The Bolsheviks' overthrow the Tsarist regime, providing justifications for this revolution, but this is only the point at which one discourse supersedes another—we are told that we cannot assume this event has anything to do with the necessity to sweep the Tsarist regime from the historical stage. Rather, necessities are imagined after the event, imposed on a chain of contingency, and are able to masquerade as progressive simply because there has been a violent occupation of the historical stage. The Bolsheviks can invent historical necessity, and convince their revolutionary adherents to accept their interpretation, simply because they have successfully replaced one discourse with another. "An event," Foucault tells us, "is not a decision, a treaty, a reign, or a battle, but the reversal of a relationship of forces, the usurpation of power, the appropriation of a vocabulary turned against those who had once used it."[16]

Hence we discover the emergence of an analysis that can speak only of contingency. Here is a demand to treat history as a series of particular ruptures, connected only to the deployment of power, that rejects *a priori* all talk of continuity and universality. Due to an almost neurotic desire to avoid totalization, this demand has done, though often unintentionally, great damage to history.

This rejection of totalization, however, and the replacement of necessity with contingency, was a

16. Michel Foucault, "Nietzsche, Genealogy, History" (http://noehernandezcortez.files.wordpress.com/2011/04/nietzsche-genealogy-history.pdf), 88.

logical response to the excesses of revisionism and crude historical materialism. The post-modern currents in thought, that along with capitalism sought to banish communism to the netherworld of theory, cannot be simply dismissed as a petty-bourgeois phenomenon, though it most certainly amounts to petty-bourgeois ideology. In some ways, such a position was also a theoretical rejoinder to an equally petty-bourgeois deformation of communism that, by the time China's revolution was reversed, was briefly hegemonic. Here was a communism that tended to understand social reality according to the crudest comprehension of social class—an understanding that might have caused even Marx to shudder—that excluded other oppressed social positions and argued that ideologies such as feminism, anti-racism, queer radicalism, etc. were little more than petty-bourgeois politics that had nothing to do with the serious business of class struggle.

Partially in response to this crude class essentialism, which was a dogmatic desire to adhere to a "pure" marxism (as if it was ever "pure"), the radical proponents of this new theoretical fad would champion the idea of disunified identity-based struggles because, sometimes influenced by their own experience, the most popular communist understanding of necessity at that time seemed incapable of pulling these other concerns into its orbit. In many ways this practice was the penalty of the sins of dogmatic and chauvinist communism, and it is worth recognizing this fact and using it as an occasion for reflection. In other words, we need to admit that it was a necessity to take these other concerns into account, to understand how they possibly determined social class, rather than dismissing them as entirely contingent.

At the same time, however, the politics produced due to the rejection of a totalizing necessity was a politics that could lead nowhere. Sites of identity-based struggles could only produce a praxis incapable of solidarity. Theories of "intersectionality" were most often banal, merely a recognition of the fact that multiple moments of oppression and exploitation, including economic class, intersect. Simply noting the possibility of intersection, though, is not an analysis; it is an ineffectual truism. These theories were thus incapable of explaining the meaning of this intersection—after all, to provide this meaning would be an act of totalization. Affinity groups, safe spaces, border wars in the names of various categories of oppression. A general theoretical chaos that could produce little more than confusion that amounted to a political limbo.

Thus necessity again rears its unpopular head, and those who would reject its logic would be entirely uncomfortable with the claim that their praxis of contingency produces also its own necessity. For here, at a point where totalization is rejected as murderous, the valorization of contingency must become entirely *necessary*. And if we examine the practice of this politics we are forced to conclude that these politics necessarily lead to the limited practice of social reformism—for what else can identity politics, which has no political content beyond valorizing sites of oppression as radical identities, produce? Not the solidarity and organization that world historical revolutions have taught us are necessary for revolution. Indeed, reformist practice is precisely the concrete result of this type of politics—its most vocal proponents, if they are active at all, are generally active primarily in struggles for social reform. The hope behind this activity, though, was the hope of movementism: that multiple sites of struggle would become more than the sum of their reformist parts, that the avalanche of multiplicity would produce a radical movement capable of eclipsing the simple unity of past practices.

This practice of combining contingency with multiplicity is probably best expressed in Deleuze and Guattari's concept of the *rhizome* that is meant to replace a revolutionary ideology based on revolutionary unity. The assumption is that such unity implies totalization, the capture of radical desire. The metaphor of a potato root spreading in innumerable directions is meant to replace the metaphor of a party with roots in the masses—how can we root ourselves in the manner of a tree if the subterranean reality is so vast? Something rhizomatic is required, capable of spreading along multiple trajectories without any apparent unity. Negri and Hart's notion of the *multitude*, first theorized in *Empire*, is a further development of this concept.

Interestingly enough, a young Badiou understood the political direction indicated by the theory of the rhizome (and hence the multitude) and was able to predict the emergence of movementism at the centres of capitalism post-1968:

> Under the anti-organizational pretexts, it is not too difficult to see the rejection of the point of view of class. Its theme was the need to add up the revolts (immigrants, women, ecologists, soldiers, prisoners, students, homosexuals, etc.) to enumerate the punctual social forces to infinity, but obstinately to combat anything resembling the political unification of the people's camp, seized in its antagonistic inflection, in its living class being. Organization and its alleged 'castrating hierarchy' make for broad targets: the One of the multiple in revolt is a question of content, of the politics of the people. Some hid behind the blunders of the form, here and there, in order to deny the content. Badly camouflaged behind the hatred of militancy was the hatred of the class struggle. [...] In effect, if the people do not have their own politics, they will

enact the politics of their enemies: the political abhors the void.[17]

Thus, in focusing on multiplicity at the expense of unity—and especially at the expense of the primary division between a unified ruling class and the exploited masses whose unity is necessitated by the unity of the former—a reification of the totality of capitalism, the politics of the enemy, is accomplished.

17. Alain Badiou, "The Fascism of the Potato" (http://www.scribd.com/doc/112405252/Alain-Badiou-The-Fascism-of-the-Potato), 1-2. What is meant, here, by "the One" versus "the Multiple", aside from being a long-standing ontological question that is tangental to this treatise, is Deleuze and Guattari's complaint that capitalism is a singularity that crushes and represses multiple expressions of identity. In this sense, any organizational unity is also a reflection of this repressive singularity, necessarily muting difference, and is thus tantamount to a conflict between two different singularities (two opposed versions of the problematized "One") that necessarily ignores the fact of multiplicity. Hence, Deleuze and Guattari's attempt to replace the materialist dialectic (the *one* of the bourgeois order divides into the *two* of proletarian versus bourgeois) with their concept of the rhizome (the division is simply two versions of totality and so it is better to conceive of resistance according to multiple lines of flight). Badiou is arguing, however, that social and historical reality does reduce, in the last instance, to a "scission" between two different positions and that the multiplicity of revolt necessarily requires unity: myriad expressions of revolt may in fact demonstrate the need for this unity. An unqualified multiplicity left to its own devices enshrines a unified bourgeois order.

Decades later we have seen the result of these politics; the anti-globalization movement shattered against the unity of the state's totality. If Badiou has since made a detour from the mindset behind the above quotation, it is only because he has also passed through a period of retreat that has affected his reassertion of the name of communism. Social being does determine social consciousness, to a significant extent, and it is doubtful that he would disagree with this axiom.

In any case, the desire to replace necessity with contingency, and unity with multiplicity, is often based on a misunderstanding of these concepts. There is a common misconception about revolutionary necessity that defines this term according to a crude enlightenment concept of linear progress: here necessity is confused with *destiny*, as if to argue for the scientific necessity of communism is identical to arguing that communism will necessarily happen, or that it is preordained by history. Thus, if necessity does indeed mean destiny then it is easy to understand why contingency is seen as preferable. No revolution is fated; the science of history is not the kind of science that automatically determines significant transformations in the mode of production.

We cannot claim, however, that communist theory has never dabbled in these simplistic and quasi-superstitious historical claims. Even the great communist leaders and theorists have been wont to argue that communism's necessity was also a destiny, an unavoidable truth produced by the argument of history. Whether or not these arguments were made for rhetorical reasons, or because those making the arguments were living at a specific historical conjuncture (socialism was already established and so communism could be seen as being on its way), ignores the fact that, regardless of this dabbling in antiquated concepts of unilinear progress, many of those who have argued for necessity have also been quite honest in their claims that this necessity might never emerge.

As noted previously, Engels claimed that the scientific strength of communist theory was based on the fact that there was a choice (and a choice is never preordained) between a communist future and a capitalist apocalypse—Rosa Luxemburg defined this choice as one between socialism or barbarism. Marx claimed that revolution was a necessity and once one speaks of revolution one must also realize that, according to Lenin, revolutions are not spontaneous events and thus the very fact of organizing a revolution undermines the concept of some unavoidable communist destiny. Mao spoke of even the stage of socialism as being a moment in the revolutionary chain that could be overthrown so that capitalism could be reestablished. To these insights we can also add the insights of innumerable marxist academics who have challenged this fated teleological interpretation of necessity for over a century.

While it is true that this unilinear concept of revolutionary progress has often been part of communist discourse, it was never properly part of revolutionary science—there is too much evidence to the contrary, regardless of the occasional and spurious claims in the polemics of its most faithful adherents. The same adherents were also known to make contrary claims, after all, even if some of their more dogmatic readers and militants focused on these throwaway lines regarding some vague notion of scientific destiny. No critical marxist devoted to the concept of necessity has truly believed in the inevitability of communism; only anti-communists and those organizations that made the mistake of accepting this rhetorical discourse believed otherwise. Necessity means only that communism is necessary to solve the problems produced by capitalism, not that its emergence is destined; water is a necessary requirement for human existence but this does not mean that every human being will have access to water simply because it is a necessity.

Theorists whose understanding of communism parallels an anti-communist discourse inherited from the cold war era continue to assert this story about necessity's synonymity with outdated concepts of unilinear, destined progress. As it would be ignorant to dismiss modern physics due to the errors of the Newtonian paradigm, it is similarly ignorant to dismiss historical materialism due to the past moments of the science that, in any case, were not as erroneous as this anti-communist narrative assumes. But such a dismissal became common sense by the end of the 20th century in first world academic and intellectual circles: totality, unity, and necessity were replaced with fragmentation, difference, and contingency.

It is in this context that the contemporary academic attempts to reclaim communism have manifested. The rejection of necessity, universality, continuity on the part of those who speak of hypotheses and horizons only makes sense if seen as a tendency to reclaim totalization in a manner that will appeal to the theoretical traditions that rejected this totalization in the first place. They desire to again speak of communism but are unable to properly engage with that history once dismissed as totalitarian. They wish to speak of universality but end up endorsing particularity in a refusal to examine necessity.

The result is a theoretical eclecticism that is only capable of producing, sometimes intentionally, movementist strategies where it is better to tail a disorganized rebellion without goals, without theoretical organization, without a coherence born from revolutionary necessity, than to coherently address the problems raised by the chain of world historical revolutions. But anarchists and left liberals can also claim these movementist rebellions, and the former camp has more reason to adopt this incoherence as an organizational principle. What does a communist analysis matter when it tells us nothing more significant than what the anarchists have been preaching since Bakunin? How does an academic assessment of communism, incapable of actually stepping outside of the framework of history-as-contingency, contribute anything theoretically significant? All of this recent and abstract talk of horizons and hypotheses is ultimately silenced by these questions. Alter the terminology in these accounts, delete the word communism, and we are back in the same anti-communist framework that these new manifestos claim to transcend.

So many of these accounts, from Foucault to the recent academic reclamations of communism, share an implicit disdain for actual revolutionary moments. In the act of disparaging revolution as either totalizing or failing to represent true liberation, they are forced to dismiss those mass movements that fought to establish a better world. Hence these academic fads, whatever their strengths, are in the last instance alien to those people, the wretched of the earth, who are still fighting for the end of capitalism.

collaboration

The dead-end of contemporary radical theory casts a shadow over any attempt to reignite anti-capitalist praxis; it is no wonder that academics speak vaguely of horizons and ideals, that intellectual groups invent fanciful terms and imaginary insurrections, and that movementism becomes the default practice. We should not be surprised that these new radicalisms that dare to speak the name communism are always fashionable amongst the academic left. It is quite normal, and even encouraged, to judge past revolutionary theory boring, predictable, and unworthy of reclamation.

When some of us speak of revisionism or opportunism, or any of those conceptual names that were understood and reasserted over-and-over by past revolutionaries, we are charged with orthodoxy. Compared to those theorists who are constantly inventing new terminologies (here, what is exciting is often defined by what is the most conceptually nebulous) we appear anachronistic, old-fashioned, out-of-step with reality. Occasionally we might be told that we are alienating people with these old concepts, as if the new concepts are any less alienating, and those responsible for such charges forget that, just decades ago, we would have been charged with the same alienating practice simply by using that old-fashioned word communism.

(Let us leave aside, for the moment, the fact that the mass revolutionary struggles at the peripheries, since the end of the 1980s to the present, draw from this supposedly "orthodox" theoretical tradition that resonates with their understanding of the world. Let us bracket the fact that this charge of being old-fashioned is also a charge levelled at every significant third world communist struggle to date — some that are happening even now — and pretend, as some radical theorists indeed pretend, that there are no struggles that matter beyond the centres of global capitalism.)

Obviously we cannot discount attempts to conceive of struggle through new concepts; it is indeed dogmatic to adhere to a pure theoretical constellation and to reject all interventions that challenge static ways of seeing the world. At the same time, as discussed, it is equally dogmatic to reject the theoretical tradition that emerged through concrete revolutionary struggle — this may be the worst form of dogmatism, in fact, because it echoes precisely what we were taught was normative by triumphalist capitalist ideology.

The question we need to ask, then, is what clarifies the current historical conjuncture, arming the masses with an ideology capable of producing revolution. None of these new manifestos, regardless of how exciting their theoretical approach looks and sounds, is capable of answering this question and thus providing a new framework for revolution. These new approaches simply reassert the same tired theoretical substitutions that have been proposed since the emergence of scientific socialism — they might sound interesting, but do little beyond the echo of their words.

Furthermore, could it be that the broad brush-strokes of revolutionary theory that emerged with Marx, passed first through Lenin and then through Mao, provide a simpler and clearer explanation of theory and practice than any of these contemporary approaches that attempt to ignore this theoretical development by classifying it as orthodox and dogmatic? This is not to say that these broad brush-strokes should ignore and dismiss the concepts of parallel traditions; the question simply has to do with what framework is capable of providing a clearer picture of reality so as to produce revolutionary action.

In these cynical days all attempts to mobilize the concepts of past revolutionary movements are treated as out-of-step with intellectual fashion. While returning to Marx is no longer unfashionable, returning to some of those theories that developed marxism through revolutionary action is in bad taste. Tiqqun and the Invisible Committee, for example, associate marxism-leninism with fascism—lazily adopting right-wing jingoism and the

wisdom of Orwell—while celebrating social chau-
vinists such as Sade and Nietzsche.[18] Despite conjuring the name of communism, it is clear that the
Invisible Committee sees those who have actually
succeeded in making revolution as their enemy. So
better to reconstruct marxism, if not a vague communism only slightly influenced by Marx (but just
Marx!), according to newer and exciting concepts,
a fanciful jargon buffet, than draw upon that tired
conceptual terrain that was judged a wasteland by
the so-called end of history.

But why should we settle for intellectual fads,
and why should the practice of revolution be confused with the business of academic fashion? Recall
that Marx and Engels broke from academic fashion and chose instead to develop and establish their
theory within working-class struggle. By doing so,
they achieved something far more significant than
they would have produced had they remained within the ivory tower circles: a theory that resonated
with those who possessed the concrete need to overthrow capitalism. And though they might have been
deemed unfashionable by the academic standards
of the time, they produced a revolutionary legacy
that eclipses whatever legacy has been left by their
once academically popular contemporaries whose

18. The Invisible Committee, *The Coming Insurrection* (Los
Angeles: Semiotext(e), 2009), 93-94.

names are only now remembered mainly *because* of Marx and Engels — Feuerbach, Stirner, Bauer, even Duhring.

None of this is to say that we should ignore the fact that the word communism has become rather unfashionable at the centres of global capitalism — this is the reason, after all, for all of these new attempts at reclamation. We should know, however, that communism is unfashionable at the imperialist centres due to decades of anti-communist propaganda combined with a privileged labour aristocracy and the aforementioned "end of history" discourse. Perhaps the desire to rebrand communism with a new language and costume is an attempt to reconstruct its popularity amongst the anti-communist "middle-class" at the centres of capitalism — a communism that sounds different but that is secretly the same as the old communism that we once rejected.

Rebranding communism, aside from the commercial logic inherent in such an approach, can only fail if it is aimed solely at that class of people who possess the privilege to wallow in the theoretical obscurantism that is offered as a replacement revolutionary theory. That is, a theory that can only be appreciated by those petty-bourgeois intellectuals who believe that conceptual opaqueness implies radicalism. Here it is important to note that even the "non-academic" theories reclaiming communism that have attained a certain level of popularity amongst the first world activist left (i.e. the Invisible Committee, Théorie Communiste, Endnotes, various autonomist marxisms, etc.) are accessible mainly to a privileged population that, even if it prides itself on having never gone to university, is still quite distant from the lived experience of the most oppressed and exploited. One of the long-standing problems with our movementist history has been the fact that the mainstream and activist left has largely been composed of people from student and/ or middle-class contexts.[19]

In any case: if these theoretical substitutions do not resonate with the lived conditions of the most exploited and oppressed, but only with those whose class outlook is somewhat elitist, then we must wonder at their revolutionary status.

We should not, however, endorse some banal anti-intellectualism and fetishize illiteracy as proletarian. Even the revolutionary theory of yesteryear might at first seem opaque now that large portions of the masses have been socialized, after decades of anti-communism, to forget the concepts that emerged from their struggles. There is that theory and an

---

19. Note that A.K. Thompson's *Black Bloc, White Riot* (Oakland: AK Press, 2010) is an attempt to examine how and why the anti-globalization movement and the mainstream activist left in Canada and the US come primarily from privileged backgrounds rather than from the ranks of the proletariat.

accompanying philosophy that, due to the complexity of the terrain, will necessarily require significant education and study to grasp—pure mathematics, theoretical physics, philosophy of logic, ontology— but none of these areas of study pretend, at least not regularly, to be theories about making revolution. Hence we should wonder at those opaque theories that did not emerge from revolutionary struggle, that were imagined by academics usually disconnected from these struggles, but claim to be the answer to the masses' quandary about making revolution.

The point, here, is not whether or not a theory is difficult to understand; this is a problem that can be solved by making education accessible to the most oppressed and exploited. Rather, whenever we encounter a new theory that speaks of overthrowing the existing social order, and claims to offer the conceptual tools for doing so, we should ask whether these tools are capable of providing a concrete analysis of concrete conditions and reflect the lived experience of the world's most exploited and oppressed.

What we often discover when we ask the above question, though, are theories that primarily speak to the lived experience of a very small and particular population based at the centres of capitalism: academics and intellectuals, activists already converted to socialism—the very lived experience of the chic theoretician who is attempting to make what was once understood as a privileged and "petty-bourgeois" social position into the basis for revolutionary action! Some of these theoreticians and their readers might even pride themselves in being "anti-intellectual" and treating academia with scorn, though the work they produce is still consumed mainly by a population divorced from those who have nothing left to lose but their chains. The most oppressed and exploited masses are reading neither Badiou nor Debord, neither Zizek nor the Invisible Committee; most of them are not even reading Marx or Lenin, Luxemburg or Mao. The difference between the former and latter categories of theory, however, is that the latter, emerging from concrete revolutionary history, does speak to the lived experience of the masses whereas the former does not. Theory alienated from practice that contrives to speak in the name of praxis should be treated with suspicion.

There is at least one answer to this problem, a way to escape the charge of academic obscurantism: more than a few of these new theorists have claimed, from the 1960s to the present, that privileged students and academics have become the new revolutionary agent—a new vanguard, but in a spontaneous sense. Middle-class children rioting in the streets of first world privilege, students versed in obscurantist jargon smashing Starbucks windows, movementist leaders familiar with the discourse of critical theory.[20] Anything to ignore the fact that these eclectic attempts to re-establish communism are entirely moribund, disconnected from what would make them truly revolutionary: an organized and militant mass movement spear-headed by the grave-diggers of capitalism.

While it is tempting for those of us who are petty-bourgeois intellectuals and students to believe that we will command the revolution—that our class privilege is more of an asset than an inhibition—we need to recognize this empty fantasy for what it is. Our class has never led revolutionary movements and has most often ended up *hampering* these movements; the theory we occasionally invent to justify our revolutionary status might be an attempt to maintain our privilege in a movement that should be aimed at ending privilege altogether. Here is a terrible notion, one that we avoid whenever we embrace those theories that justify our class privilege: we will more than likely be *sent down to the countryside*, whatever this figurative "countryside" happens to be; we too will have to be reeducated. Most of us are terrified by this possibility, disgusted by the necessity of rectification, of being dragged down.

---

20. See, for example, the aforementioned book by A.K. Thompson, *Black Bloc, White Riot: Antiglobalization and the Genealogy of Dissent*, which is a perfect example of this discourse.

We need to recognize, however, that being dragged down to the level of the masses is at the same time a *dragging up* of the masses to a level that, under the current state of affairs, only some are privileged enough to occupy. To reject this radical moment of equalization is to reify class, to believe that even after a revolution we are superior to those who were not given our opportunities, to act as if the necessity of revolutionary levelling is akin to oppression. Just as Dante descended into Hell in order to climb to Heaven, recognizing in this descent that Hell was the world in reverse, communism can only be achieved through a painful and chaotic descent of those who have the most to lose—a descent paralleled by the ascent of that class that had nothing to lose but its chains.

It is interesting to note that the most prevalent left-wing anti-intellectualism—where critical literacy itself is treated as bourgeois—generally maintains the same elitism. By placing value on some imagined authentic proletarian intelligence and culture, it argues against the necessity for mass education and mass reeducation. These anti-intellectual tendencies implicitly assume that the "dragging up" is elitist because it is secretly fearful of being dragged down. The proletariat must stay true to this imaginary essence, to its supposedly illiterate consciousness, that is understood as beautiful in its ignorance of anything but its spontaneous revolutionary values. The intellectual division of labour remains, cloaked by a clumsy attempt to argue that some illiterate but authentic "working class culture" (as if the proletariat possesses a homogenous culture) should be preserved. This class culturalism tends to be promoted by those people who already possess intellectual privilege; this politics is an attempt to replace theories of *declassing* with a quasi-theory of patronization.

Instead of tendering new theories, new ways to package communism, we need to confront our historical inability to address the anti-communist ideology that has become prevalent at the centres of capitalism: we collaborated with our silence, we accepted the bourgeois discourse of failure, we refused to organize and share our education, and we hid within the abyss of academic privilege, withdrawing from struggle, allowing communism to become an unfashionable term. We collaborated and still collaborate with every lie promoted about the late Soviet Union or the pre-Deng Communist China and their supposed crimes against humanity—falsely compared to fascism due to a discourse of "totalitarianism" that we have also, out of fear and ignorance, supported. We collaborated when we chose to tail rebellions, refusing to organize them into anything militantly coherent, out of the fear that the masses were not ready for revolution. We collaborate when we refuse to recognize the ongoing communist people's wars at the peripheries of global capitalism and refuse to transpose this experience into our own concrete circumstances. We collaborate when we dismiss the demands of necessity, embrace some banal notion of contingency, and refuse to speak of communism as anything other than an abstract ideal.

language idealism

Academic collaboration reaches its nadir when it sinks into a vague language idealism. Here is where the concept of communism is misunderstood as a Platonic form. Here is where the concrete politics of this concept are reduced to a language game and the necessity of revolution is abandoned.

When some theorists claim that communism is a notion that can be projected into the distant past as an idea or hypothesis that was always present, then the revolutionary articulation of this name that was first provided by Marx and Engels—and thus meant something different from the name that was used, if it was used, in prior epochs—is dismissed. Names are conflated with concepts and a concept that could only emerge at the end of the 19th century, regardless of the etymological cipher used to earmark this concept, is suddenly imagined to have existed prior to the only moment in which it could have emerged.

The word communism is thus dissected according to a vague notion, dislocated from what it meant when it was used by Marx and Engels, and can be misunderstood as transhistorical and *a priori*: there were always movements that believed in *community*, in holding *property in common*—why not pretend that the crude and utopian socialisms of the early Christians were conceptually the same as the scientific socialism expounded by Marx and Engels? The answer should be evident, though its simplicity might appear at first glance to be too vulgar to be accepted: Marx and Engels went to great lengths to demonstrate the difference of their socialism from the utopian socialisms of their time and thus named it as communist so as to not simply use the word *socialist* that was also being used by the utopians. As such, they were not at all interested in using this word as it had been used in the past, regardless of the vague conceptual similarities the name evoked.

And yet academic collaborators have consistently obsessed over a name, confusing the moment of naming with the moment of conceptualization. Jean-Luc Nancy's essay "Communism, the Word" is paradigmatic of this language idealism: here is an instance where a philosopher uses some vague notion of etymological destiny to confuse names with concepts. Communism as a word is traced back to the 11th and 14th centuries; some similarities between the modern conception and the nebulous premodern conception are established ("people having in common" and "common property" and ultimately "being-in-common"), and then the modern, revolutionary notion is dismissed because of an inability to adhere to the name's supposed etymological roots. The end result? "Communism, therefore, means the common condition of all the singularities of subjects, that is of all the exceptions, all the uncommon points whose network makes a world... It does not belong to the political."[21] A vague and nebulous definition, designed to exclude the revolutionary definition, based on an etymological game that takes the Latin *communitas* as its point of departure. When meaning is located in etymology, any conceptualization of the word that does not strictly cohere to its etymological origins is treated as erroneous.

But Marx and Engels did not employ the name communism because they sought fidelity with an esoteric and etymological meaning; it was simply one word, chosen amongst many, to define a scientific concept that, during their time, was entirely new and in search of a name. They could have used other words, if they had so chosen, and only used the word communism because it appeared to represent

---

21. Jean-Luc Nancy, "Communism, the Word" (http://www.lacan.com/essays/?page_id=126).

what they meant. And what they meant was a concept, not simply a name, but a concept to which this name is now irrevocably attached. As Engels wrote in 1885:

Communism among the French and Germans, Chartism among the English, now no longer appeared as something accidental which could just as well not have occurred. These movements now presented themselves as a movement of the modern oppressed class, the proletariat, as the more or less developed forms of its historically necessary struggle against the ruling class, the bourgeoisie; as forms of the class struggle, but distinguished from all earlier class struggles by this one thing, that the present-day oppressed class the proletariat, cannot achieve its emancipation without at the same time emancipating society as a whole from division into classes and, therefore, from class struggles. And Communism now no longer meant the concoction, by means of the imagination, of an ideal society as perfect as possible, but insight into the nature, the conditions and the consequent general aims of the struggle waged by the proletariat.[22]

---

22. Friedrich Engels, *On The History of the Communist League* (http://www.marxists.org/archive/marx/works/1847/communist-league/1885hist.htm).

To speak of some inner communist truth based on a recourse to language games is ultimately disingenuous: it tells us nothing of the conceptual terrain opened by those theorists who were arguing for the necessity of revolutionary science. Although one is always welcome to embrace the meanings of names before the emergence of a coherent concept, this recourse to an eternal idea/hypothesis or etymological essence is an abandonment of history.

For if etymology determines conceptual destiny then every science is non-sensical. Modern particle physics, after all, utilizes the word *atom* and only the anti-scientific ignorant would dare to argue that today's physicists are committing a grave error by failing to adhere to that word's etymological roots. To suggest that the modern scientist remain faithful to the original ancient Hellenic conceptualization of the name "atom" in order to properly understand their science is laughable at best. At worst it is reactionary.

Words in any language are mediated by the historical moment. Words are not substances; they do not possess intrinsic essences. Concepts stand over and above words, though they often use specific names that communicate some sort of vague meaning to the concept—such a meaning, though, is demonstrated by a succession of *a posteriori* words designed to further demarcate a concept. We are indeed limited by our language, but this language is not in and of itself a destiny. Etymological analysis is useful to explain a given word's origin but it does not decide conceptual meaning. As Wittgenstein once claimed, "the meaning of a word is its use in language."[23] And since marxists believe that a given language is in the last instance the product of concrete history, and that language is always mediated by social and historical circumstances, we must go further and claim that the meaning of a word is determined by concrete social processes.

After all, this attempt to locate the meaning of the word in its historical point of origin immediately becomes non-sensical, and even eurocentric, once we take into account communities that do not share the same grammatical history. Communists in India, Nepal, and Afghanistan, for example, do not have the etymological concept of *communitas*—a Latin word—from which to derive the modern concept of *communism* that, for them, is precisely the concept originally theorized by Marx and Engels. Does this mean that they do not properly understand this concept because it belongs to those language communities who share Latin and Greek as their grammatical roots? Obviously not. Even worse, does this mean that they are importing a concept that, due to the Latin origins of its name, is itself a eurocentric

---

23. Ludwig Wittgenstein, *Philosophical Investigations* (Oxford: Blackwell, 1997), I § 43.

imposition on their own struggles—clearly Badiou's form of language idealism would deny this etymological tendency since, quite obviously, we can find utopian "communist" practices in these non-European spaces as well. Contrary to Badiou's assumption, though, these early practices, like those elsewhere, were not at all the same practices as the clear-cut theoretical *and scientific* concept at the end of the nineteenth century. Just as one cannot project capitalism back into the ancient world, one can also not project communism into the pre-capitalist past.[24]

Moving from the heights of academia to the still alienated theory of popular leftist intellectuals, we find the same language idealism amongst the communism of the Invisible Committee, Théorie Communiste, Endnotes, and others. The movementist activist circles that are interested again in the name of communism are probably not reading Nancy, but they are gravitating to these chic communization theorists, or at least the most popular

---

24. Of course, Marx and Engels did use the term "primitive communism" when they examined the early history of humanity, but they were quite clear that they were reading these past societies through the lens of the present. They were also clear that those early modes of production were not conceptually identical to their contemporary communism. Moreover, limited as they were to ethnocentric anthropological accounts, it may not be wise to accept much of what they wrote about "primitive communism" as scientifically valid.

expressions of autonomism, and in doing so are being introduced to a concept of communism that is primarily based on its etymological roots: community, reclaiming the commons, and anything that can divorce the word from how it developed through the most revolutionary moments of the 20th century.

Any reclamation of the word communism, then, cannot be a reclamation that relies only on this amorphous academic exercise which attempts to locate meaning outside of concrete historical practices and instead obsesses over names and vague utopian articulations that preceded the most coherent and contemporary variant of the concept. Concepts are not transhistorical but are produced by humans living in real social and historical circumstances.

We should ask what practices this type of language idealism necessitates. Since such theories reject the concrete in favour of nebulous proclamations, they cannot produce a concretely revolutionary project. Their radicalism becomes little more than a theoretical gesture.

chapter three:
new returns

If we are to speak of a new return to revolutionary communism then we must first think through the problem of an *old return*. Having so far rejected all of the rearticulations of communism that attempt to distance the name from the conceptual content of its history, it would be easy to assume that this treatise is advocating a return to the way communism was conceptualized and practiced before the "end of history" was declared. Such an assessment would be simultaneously true and false.

On the one hand, it is true that this book is advocating a return to an understanding of communism that has been distanced from the contemporary renewal of its name. Against the rise of post-modernism and chic radical theories, we have examined a return to the recognition of revolutionary science and its truth procedures, developed and established through a dialectic of success and failure, that resulted in a rich theoretical terrain. Such a terrain is far more useful for revolutionary practice, for making sense of the world so as to transform it, than contemporary movementist communism; the former should not be rejected due to a cold war ideology that has socialized us into thinking of it only as catastrophe. Moreover, there is an ahistorical discourse that has produced a totalized representation of past communist movements and theories: it is quite common to encounter the argument, made particularly by post-modernists and post-colonialists, that the marxism of the past could not theorize anything other than a crude and eurocentric notion of social class.

On the other hand, this treatise is not arguing for a return to a communism that is unaware of the developments of social and theoretical struggle that have taken place since the end of the 1980s: this is not a demand to return to the particular communism that was practiced directly after the October Revolution in 1917, or even to the particular communism that was practiced in the course of the Chinese Revolution under Mao. The most obvious problem of making such a demand is the fact that these revolutions *did* fail. And though we should not comprehend these failures according to an end of history discourse that forbids memory—we should recognize that there were important truths established in these revolutions, hard-won by the struggles of past revolutionaries—we should not fetishize the possibility of perfect repetition.

There is a rather dogmatic way of assessing our revolutionary past: failures are attributed to a lack of fidelity to the perfect theory of making revolution, the result of the errors of individuals and the organizations they controlled. The solution, by that logic, would be to repeat precisely what allowed these revolutions to happen but with attention to a proper and "pure" understanding of theory. Is this not the rallying cry of every marginal trotskyist sect? "If only comrade Trotsky had been in charge of the Bolsheviks after Lenin; the revolution was ruined when Stalin bastardized a perfectly good revolutionary theory!" As noted in the previous chapters, however, there is no pure communist theory just as there is no pure science. An absolutist conceptualization of science is one in which scientific truths cannot be challenged by successive experiments; this is a science closed to the future and, due to this closure, dogmatic rather than scientific. The concept of necessity explains why this is the case: encounters with historical necessity demand that we establish ruptural truths in continuity with an unfolding truth procedure. Hence, we must maintain the same standard of assessment when we engage with the terrain of revolutionary theory and practice; we must assert that there is no ideal communism to which we can ever return. There are no precise formulae but there are universal axioms. It is easy to conflate these two categories and end up either fetishizing or dismissing the concepts developed throughout the history of revolutionary struggle.

Many of us can easily recall those ortho-communists who frequent activist demonstrations, actions, teach-ins, and panels. Missionaries of a communism that belongs to the first two decades of the 20th century, these tragic individuals deliver the same interventions and denunciations at every event where they are permitted to speak. The same formula is given with little attention to the event's particular context: "the solution is for the working-class to unite and overthrow capitalism." Often this formula is meant as a denunciation because these unimaginative persons are under the impression that nobody in attendance has ever thought about unity or the overthrow of capitalism; their assumption is based perhaps on the fact that these events concern Palestinian self-determination, or the role of politics in art, or a current example of state repression. Indeed, perhaps another reason many of us did not wish to identify with communism in the past was because we mistakingly associated it with those fringe dogmatists who were incessantly repeating vague claims about working-class unity based on a working-class that was clearly imaginary because, according to all empirical evidence, these "comrades" did not represent the interests of the masses in whose name they spoke.

We should be able to recognize such an old return to communism as a return that is ultimately conservative. Learning nothing of how struggle has developed since 1917 to the present—filtering nearly a century of history through unyielding categories of thought that in fact deform history so as to remain ignorant despite a veneer of savvy "know-how"—this practice of communism lacks vitality. Of course, it is correct to argue that the solution is to unify the proletariat so as to overthrow capitalism, but this is a slogan that deals only with the last instance and, as Althusser never tired of reminding us, the last instance often never arrives. How many historical moments and sites of struggle operate so as to mediate this truism about working-class unity and force us to ask about the meaning of unity, the composition and definition of the working-class, the precise strategy of overthrowing capitalism? What does this sloganeering have to do with every particular event that may be talking about something that is also vital, and also connected to class struggle? Formulaic maxims, after all, tend to shut down our ability to understand the content of particular sites of struggle. So why is it that these individuals often assume that many of these other instances of social struggle, mainly because they do not resemble a doctrinaire definition of praxis, are not themselves about class unity and the overthrow of capitalism? In other words, could these marxist conservatives actually be opposing concrete class struggle by mystifying the debate according to an idealized definition of the proletariat and bourgeoisie? We could ask more rhetorical questions but there is no point; most of us are viscerally repelled by the idea of becoming this kind of cliched marxist—it is as compelling as becoming a Mormon.

Let us go further, leaving behind these tragic communist conservatives, and think through the fact of communist catastrophe. We should have no problem admitting that past communist movements did end in catastrophe. These were catastrophes not for the reasons provided by various anti-communist narratives, rather the trauma was due to the very fact of the earth-shaking successes they established. That is, the failures of both the Russian and Chinese Revolutions were catastrophic because they fell from such great heights—they had accomplished so much, unleashing the world historical potential of the masses only to collapse. Whereas capitalism is a catastrophe because of its successes, communism was a catastrophe because its successes were overthrown by its eventual failures. It is not tragic that capitalism is catastrophic because it is not a failure on the part of capitalism; according to its internal logic it does precisely what it is meant to do—exploitation, commodification, over-accumulation, etc. Indeed, the problem is not that capitalism "doesn't work" (as some anti-globalization slogans would have us think) but that it works very well.[25] Past experiences of communism, however, have been tragic in the same way that Oedipus, Antigone, and Hamlet are tragic: we celebrate them and mourn the ways in which they have been laid low.

And yet communism is not a tragic hero that, upon dying, can never be recovered except in the literary epic. Communism's tragedy is due to the fact of historical necessity: it is always open to the future, reversed upon each new return that seeks to reignite the greatness that was overwhelmed by historical problems it could not anticipate—a

---

25. To be fair, there are those utopian capitalists who are enamoured with Ayn Rand, Adam Smith's invisible hand, and other unscientific understandings of capitalism who actually do believe that capitalism is not working in the way it was intended to work. These are speculative fantasies and poor definitions of capitalism that are forced to rely on a vague and supernatural definition of the market. Most successful capitalists are realists who understand very well the meaning of capitalism. These realists also have their ideologues, hard-minded "pragmatists" who scoff at the utopianism of their libertarian peers, whose only moral value is in their honesty. Thomas Friedman, for example, has argued that the market's invisible hand also requires an invisible fist.

seeking that proceeds by grasping the meaning of this greatness and what led to its tragedy. By accepting what truths were established, what errors produced catastrophe, each moment of communist necessity can possibly establish new truths and encounter successive failures. Hence the Bolsheviks under Lenin overcame the failures of the Second International under Kautsky and Bernstein. Hence the Communist Party of China under Mao overcame the failures of the Third International under Stalin and Khrushchev.

We do no favours to the revolutionary masses' past sacrifices by acting as if this past is either beyond reproach or utterly reprehensible. To speak of a new return is to speak of a way in which to make sense of revolutionary history through the lived experience of the present. Moreover, all of the questions raised by those radical theories that have rejected this revolutionary past need to be answered by this new return rather than dismissed.

To speak of a new return is to recognize that the past always returns through the present. We need to recognize this return rather than allowing it to speak through our unconscious actions. History has its revenge, and it is not worth quoting that annoying Santayana platitude—of which even conservatives make much ado—to recognize this point. Marx already recognized the same point in the course of thinking through social movements where history might indeed repeat as tragedy and farce. To be unaware of the weight of dead generations is to repeat all of the mistakes of the past. Movementism has been doing this for decades; communism cannot afford to make the same error.

So if we are to think through the possibility of a new return we must also think through the way in which such a new return emerged, at the centres of capitalism, in the recent past and, following this investigation, remember the ways in which there have also been new returns to all of the erroneous practices that could prevent us from pursuing a similar return now—or even in the future when the same mistakes are repeated. Anti-revisionism and the New Left, all of the reformist traps, the false promises of speculative theory, and finally the return to groundless utopian communisms wherein the necessity of a new anti-revisionism can be discovered.

anti-revisionism

In the past generations of revolutionary struggle at the centres of capitalism there arose a New Left that also attempted to reconfigure communist ideology: the Soviet revolution was approaching the moment of revisionism and, due to this approach, some argued for the need to return to the foundations of marxism for a reassessment of revolutionary philosophy. Both the Frankfurt School and the Situationists, to name two significant examples of early New Left theorists, argued for this return and, in the course of making this argument, defended the need for an academic reassessment of revolutionary science.

These academic rapprochements, because they began as theories without practice, were largely incapable of recognizing those movements that were also calling the current state of revolutionary praxis into question but were doing so in a manner that ignored the cautious academic insights of the New Left. For the New Left did not really grasp the significance of the Chinese Revolution just as it began without a concrete understanding of the innumerable anti-colonial revolutions influenced by that world historical event in China.

While this initially academic regroupment argued for a theoretically compelling (but practically banal) reboot of marxian philosophy, an "other left"—the left of the peripheries, the revolutions beyond the scope of academic civility—demanded a return to the revolutionary marxism that was considered uncouth but, in this return, also a theoretical development beyond the limits reached by the Soviets. Where the New Left lapsed into critiques of totalitarianism in an effort to produce a marxist philosophy that could escape the traps of actually existing socialism, this other left theorized a continuity with the banned science that, in the moment of continuity, would necessitate a further point of rupture. The former group's initial dismissal of the approach taken by the latter was not simply academic: Horkheimer became a conservative reactionary. Adorno refused to take a principled stance on the Vietnam War and insultingly compared the anti-imperialist student movement (that would birth the Red Army Fraction and other urban guerrilla movements) to the Hitler Youth.

And yet the New Left also produced a variety of committed militants and tendencies, paradigmatically exemplified by the Students for a Democratic Society [SDS] and the Weather Underground Organization [WUO]. These militant currents attempted to implement the concepts of New Left academic theorists despite the fact that some of these initial theorists might have been horrified by such militancy. Here we discover tentative steps towards a radical anti-imperialism, influenced also by Ho Chi Minh and Che Guevera, that was significant in that it necessitated further radicalization.[26] In this sense, the New Left produced and intersected with

---

26. A good exploration of New Left anti-imperialism, its limits and influences, is Chris Marker's film essay, *A Grin Without A Cat*.

a variety of important political tendencies: the early feminist movement, small urban guerrilla groupings, and even a unity with Black Nationalism.[27]

It was in this context that the so-called "New Communist Movement", the anti-revisionism of yesteryear, emerged throughout the centres of capitalism. Against the limitations of the New Left, these anti-revisionists raised the demand for a new return to the dialectic of actually existing revolution; against a retreat into student politics or a flirtation with Guevarist militancy, they defended the very concepts that some sections of the New Left had claimed were out-of-date, producing a period of struggle that, in some ways, went beyond the theoretical and practical output of the New Left.[28]

---

27. I do not locate any of the struggles for New Afrikan and indigenous self-determination within the New Left because I am of the opinion that these revolutionary struggles belonged to peripheries within the global centres. Thus, they followed a logic that was exterior to the New Left, though some of the more radical New Left factions would unite with them, that had to do with dynamics of imperial and colonial oppression.

28. I am not arguing, here, that there is nothing useful in the theory and philosophy produced even by the academic representatives of the New Left. Indeed, I think that there were important aspects of this theory that, regardless of its problems, was useful in theorizing the possibility of a marxism that could be critical of the Soviet Union, that was becoming revisionist at the time, without taking an orthodox trotskyist line. Moreover, even some of the early New Left academics' engagement with culture is still relevant. In this sense, it is

Although many of these anti-revisionist militants were once trained in the discourse of the New Left, and indeed learned from some of its useful insights, they attempted to discard the limitations of this discourse in the face of revolutionary necessity.

Thus, when judged according to the standard of revolution, the New Communist Movement should be considered significant, though also limited by historical necessity. If the contributions of the New Communist Movement are generally forgotten by those who continue to adore the theoretical precedents for the New Left, it is because the latter were better preserved in academic discourse. Academia has a long institutional memory; universities control libraries and sites of publication, the ability to freeze the thought of its favoured intellectuals in time and reproduce, when it is necessary, the popular academic books of a past decade. The militants of the New Communist Movement, however, did not control printing presses or journals; most of their publications were pamphlets, programmes,

---

interesting to note that the Red Army Fraction was somewhat influenced by Herbert Marcuse's *One Dimensional Man*, one of the iconic works of the New Left. I also believe it is important to recognize the contributions of the members of the SDS and WUO, particularly since some of the members of the latter group, who involved themselves in even more militant struggle, are still in prison due to the sacrifices they made in the 1960s/70s (i.e. David Gilbert and others).

self-published books.

When the anti-revisionism of that time collapsed, the contributions of this vanishing movement, published by organizations that had ceased to exist, suddenly became scarce.[29] Academia does not have to deal with this impediment since it is also a bourgeois institution; it can republish the work of its popular leftists, sell publication rights to other established presses, and propagate the thought of an intellectual movement that at one time had been outpaced. The ideas of the New Left will continue to resonate in academia, but the terrain in which the theory of the New Communist Movement resonated—the terrain of concrete class struggle—is a space that has been largely cleansed, for various reasons, of the revolutionary theory of the past generation.

In this context, academia even preserves the memory of thinkers who were marginal to the New Left, let alone unimportant and completely disconnected from the popular social struggles of the time. For example, we can find contemporary academic leftists citing Hal Draper, a rather unremarkable thinker whose "socialism from below" is a better slogan than it is a theory, but dismissing all of the possibly exciting theoretical developments of

29. Many of these publications, however, can now be accessed online at the Encyclopedia of Anti-Revisionism Online (https://www.marxists.org/history/erol/).

the New Communist Movement since this movement operated largely outside of the boundaries of academia.

So if history repeats itself, then we can understand the current academic fad according to the vicissitudes of the past: those who speak of communist hypotheses and horizons are the "new left" of today, another generation of academics alienated from class struggle who are attempting to refocus our intention on a supposedly new and fresh approach to communism. At the same time, however, some of the activists who have been radicalized by the new left of today are already, like their historical antecedents, overstepping the initial limitations of this popular left discourse, and slowly gravitating towards a contemporary version of anti-revisionism.

We should be clear, though, about the limits of this previous cycle of anti-revisionism. The New Communist Movement was in part responsible for its own demise. In its attempt to militantly uphold anti-revisionism, many of this movement's organizations tended to offer formulaic theoretical solutions culled from past revolutionary texts or official statements from the Communist Party of China; in its desire to actively pursue communism's necessity it would eventually become distracted by sectarian squabbles. There is no reason to repeat its mistakes; lingering organizations and parties from this period that have not disintegrated are proof of that period's limitations—insular, declining, and often quite cultish.

Rather, a new phase of anti-revisionism at the centres of capitalism is required, one that is already in the process of emergence. Such a phase must begin by aligning itself with those revolutionary movements that are producing people's wars and, in these productive moments, also producing the germ of revolutionary theory. Now, in the very moment that this generation's new left is publishing treatises on the reclamation of communism, and thus beginning to overstep its own horizon, we can glimpse the dawn of an anti-revisionism that will again eclipse those radical academics who, in imagining that they are embarking upon the uncharted seas of new theory, are unconsciously repeating all of the errors of their predecessors.

the electoral trap

Thankfully many of today's new communisms are anti-revisionist enough to reject the electoral system. Some of them are notable for recognizing the uselessness of even participating in the spectre of contemporary state-sanctioned elections: Badiou has disparaged bourgeois elections, claiming

that should be rejected entirely.[30]   The Invisible
Committee claims "that it's only *against voting itself*
that people continue to vote."[31]   According to some
of these contemporary reclamations, we are at least
on an anti-revisionist trajectory. We should expect
nothing less; we should even wonder why there are
still communist parties and marxist organizations
that run in elections, attempt to enter bourgeois
parties, and base their entire strategy on an *a priori*
assumption that there can be a peaceful co-existence
with capitalism.

Anarchists have always been more militant in
their rejection of state conventions, though not always for the right reasons, and so the rejection of
the electoral trap on the part of those reclamations
of communism that approach anarchism might not
be surprising. Rather, it is when we find anarchists
talking about electoral practice as a valid tactic that
we are surprised.

There are also those amongst today's new left,
militants of a new reclamation of communism, that
find such a rejection irresponsible. To be fair, this
charge of irresponsibility is not premised on the
doctrine of "peaceful co-existence"—all of those
busy reclaiming communism for a new generation
at least recognize that communism cannot be voted

---

30. Alain Badiou, *Polemics* (London: Verso, 2006), 75-97.

31. The Invisible Committee, *The Coming Insurrection*, 23.

into reality—but simply on the assumption that we should not abandon any terrain of social struggle. If one party is capable of defending social welfare better than another, it is argued, then it is our responsibility to push them into power while continuing to struggle beyond the limits of the framework of social democracy.

Old arguments are wrenched from particular social and historical contexts in order to justify the practice of pragmatic electoral participation. Despite all efforts to kick the supposedly antiquated terminology of marxism-leninism out the door, it returns through the window—but stripped of its revolutionary vitality. Sometimes the old slur of "ultra-leftism" is used, but with anxiety and embarrassment. Those who reject everything Lenin wrote about opportunism and organization are wont to fall back on his argument regarding electoral participation in Britain, in the early decades of the 20th century, and the "infantile" nature of refusal. Hence Lenin becomes authoritative only in reference to electoral pragmatism. But if he has been dismissed as an authority in every other context, why should we bother to conjure his ghost in this particular area? Perhaps we are haunted by everything we have abandoned and thus cling to those aspects of the past that justify our behaviour in the here and now.

To treat elections as a viable space of struggle now, decades following the ascendancy of a discourse that proclaimed the capitalist end of history, is a grand act of cynicism. This cynicism is one that is already aware that it is not viable to assume that communism can be voted into existence: we know that elections do not matter, and that capitalism continues its murderous onslaught, regardless of what party is in power. To waste time and energy, then, in a struggle that will not move us any closer to our distant horizon is to participate in a convention we recognize as fraudulent. It is a bit like an unemployed biologist who pays the bills, and maintains some sort of influence over their students, by teaching six-day creationism at a private religious school.

By rejecting the theories of organization and strategy born of necessity, we are often only capable of struggling in those reformist spaces that the current social order considers legitimate. We know nothing else; an imagination of practice has atrophied. Movementism as a whole promotes such a strategy: in lieu of the coming insurrection, lurking beyond that unapproachable horizon, and instead of building a militantly structured organizational force, we might as well busy ourselves with damage control within the framework of the current state of affairs. At the very least we can achieve more results, no matter how paltry, in the space of bourgeois democracy than we can in the odd demonstration or radical parade. Seattle and Quebec City produced nothing but spectacle. Years after the Arab Spring and Occupy, the might of capitalism and imperialism are as strong as ever. Perhaps we believe that if we are able to vote into power someone who is even marginally sympathetic to our politics, regardless of whether or not they actually do anything, then we can be successful at something, even if it is merely the success of getting a politician elected.[32]

Here, it is worth wondering whether this cynical and pragmatic understanding of parliamentarianism is better than the old left's revisionist illusions about participating in the bourgeois electoral system. While it is tempting to argue that the cynical approach is refreshingly honest, it is likely that the other approach is more honest in that it is not participating in deceit. Indeed, those old communist parties that still run candidates in various elections do not recognize the contradiction of their practice; they have various rhetorical strategies and dogmas that allow them to believe that they are engaged in

---

32. To be fair, at the peripheries of global capitalism there are times when the participation in elections may occasionally be tactically useful (i.e. proving to the UN that a revolutionary grouping does have mass support) or simply the result of a real defeatism on the part of a shattered left (i.e. after decades of surviving imperialist-backed death squads, there may be nothing left for a fractured left to do, in lieu of a strong movement, but vote against reactionaries). This treatise, though, since it concerns the phenomenon of movementism, is devoted primarily to an analysis of electoral practice at the imperialist centres.

revolutionary practice and represent the will of the proletariat. One only needs to argue for an hour with an average member of the Communist Party USA or the Communist Party of Canada or the Communist Party of India (Marxist) or any other similar organization to realize that this is the case — they will accuse you of being a counter-revolutionary and in league with the bourgeoisie mainly because you challenge their political direction. They truly believe that they can vote communism into existence, or at the very least organize primarily within bourgeois democracy. Those who believe this is an illusion, however, and sublimate their energy in electoral pragmatism cannot defend their practice with such a fantastical doctrine.

But what other options, our pragmatist might argue, do we have while waiting for the communist horizon and the next convergence of movement forces? The answers come quickly, perhaps too quickly, since they have been the answers for decades: rebuild a new left that is better than the old left, embed oneself within the struggles of trade-unions.

the refoundationalist trap

Rather than establishing a movement theoretically unified in revolutionary necessity—that is, establishing the kernel of a revolutionary party of a new type—a common tendency is to instead establish projects, processes, networks, and assemblies that attempt to unify vague and fractured elements of the left that tend to resist, once they are thrown together, an over-arching clarity or unity. Assuming (and often correctly) that the left is dead, this *refoundationalism* asserts that the left's "death" is precisely the death that was declared by capitalism and that, in order to live again, the left must be rebuilt from the ground up. The strategy is to gather all the elements of moribund left grouplets into one grouping and hope that something greater than the sum of its parts will emerge from this process of gathering.

Here is yet another horizon projected into the distant future, a hypothesis that will magically be solved by mixing together people and groups who appear to share the same ideology. Again, there is nothing new to this approach, regardless of what some of its defenders might claim, and this refoundationalism often encourages movementist practice. When a variety of organizations with competing ideologies and strategies are gathered together under one banner, the only theoretical unity that can be achieved is the most vague anti-capitalism. Since revolutionary strategy is derived from revolutionary unity, the vagueness of theory produces a vagueness in practice: tailism, neo-reformism, nebulous movementism.

Refoundationalism produces a variety of tactics: university talk-shops where representatives of different movements are invited to debate in closed spaces where the left gathers to watch the left talk about the left; websites that advertise themselves as a revolutionary process; city assemblies filled with organizations that dislike each other. The aim is to produce the foundation of a new anti-capitalist movement that will somehow cohere from innumerable incoherent elements.

The problem with this approach is not the belief that, due to past failures, a new revolutionary movement needs to be built and developed, but the assumption that the historical basis of such a movement must be entirely refounded. For this assumption carries with it the groundless hope that those involved in refoundationalist projects will not bring all of the errors with them, will not be invested in the ideologies of their own failed organizations, and that the refoundationalist project as a whole will not be yet another repetition of the past and similar attempts. We know what happened to the last attempted New Left and its refoundationalist projects: it was eclipsed and swept aside by a radical anti-revisionism.

Historical necessity teaches us that the kernel of a militant organization, unified according to revolutionary theory, is the only thing capable of refounding a revolutionary movement. And this movement will grow by proving itself to the masses and thus by organizing the masses according to their emancipatory demands—not by tailing them, not by manufacturing a disunified organization out of already existent component parts, some of which do not fit together. The great revolutions of history teach us that we cannot produce an organization capable of fighting capitalism if we are building an organization that has little hope of producing a clear political line out of its confusion.

Indeed, history should have taught us that *to control the political line is to determine the movement.* Inversely, to have an indeterminate movement is to lose control of the political line. And when a movement is based on an indeterminate politics, however broadly anti-capitalist, those organizations who possess the most coherent political line will be those who end up redirecting and determining the organization, whatever its initial intent. Most often this means that some version of "common sense" ideology will triumph in these spaces: in the absence of ideological coherence, we often fall back on the way we have been socialized to understand the world and thus reformism will trump revolution.[33]

While it is true that political lines are never static (the fact of line struggle means that they are essentially dynamic) they must aim for more coherence and direction than a vague anti-capitalism that lacks clarity in theory and practice. Theoretical unity is itself a process—revolutionary parties are themselves processes—and it is thus strange to pretend, as some do, that we must have a refoundationalist process in order to produce a party, as if the party is the end result of a process rather than being the process in itself. Begin with a political line and

---

33. We do not have to work very hard to find historical examples that prove this problematic: Occupy was easy prey for liberal trade unions and reformist organizations; the Quebec Student Strike was ultimately determined by the Parti Quebecois and, to a lesser extent, Quebec Solidaire. None of this is to say, however, that we should not embrace these rebellions when they erupt, only that we should not liquidate our political line in these spaces. What is required, here, is an organizational apparatus that can circulate within every rebellion that necessarily erupts under capitalism so as to gather the advanced elements of these rebellions according to its line. Refoundationalist projects, by their very nature, are incapable of acting in such a manner. More often than not, as every refoundationalist attempt has proven so far, they simply end up getting swept up in these rebellions—provided they even participate—without a clear political line beyond a vague anti-capitalist sentiment.

demonstrate its efficacy in concrete class struggle: we prove nothing by forming new organizations with the already organized left rather than organizing the currently unorganized.

Those committed to the refoundationalist strategy, however, believe that they are involved in revitalizing the left and it is unlikely that this belief—which is little more than a dogma—will disappear anytime soon. Even the most radical refoundationalist projects who dare to speak the names of Lenin and Mao discover the limitations of the boundaries they have drawn: they too will tail the masses, will fail to pursue necessity, will always be staring at some distant horizon that will never arrive because they are not interested in making it arrive. A new anti-revisionism is required—not a new refoundationalism, not another New Left, but a new return to the communist necessity.

the trade-union trap

Another appropriate organizational practice upon which to embark while awaiting the communist horizon—and one that can be simultaneous with and even amount to reformism and refoundationalism—is union organizing. Being an old practice, long pre-dating movementism and today's reclaimed communism, there is a compelling tradition to unionism, an assumption that it can be revolutionary based on its history and already existent organization: we do not have to think about what it means to pursue the larger questions of necessity when we submerge ourselves in the day-to-day economic struggles of unionized workers, or even when we spend our energy fighting to establish a union. All we need to think about is the union, and the particular goals of the union, and not what lurks beyond the limits of this logic.

Movementism finds its home in today's trade-unionism because unions are social movements that, along with other social movements, might participate in the coming insurrection, the communist horizon. The limits of trade-union consciousness described famously by Lenin, and one of the foundational concepts behind any necessity of a revolutionary party, can be dismissed in a cavalier manner, justified by the abstract assumption that unions represent the most organized elements of the exploited masses. Past theories regarding unions as the basis of revolutionary struggle can be rebranded in the name of a movementist communism.

This is why Draperism has been revived. There is no need to build a communist organization since the working classes are already organized in unions, Draper argued, and this prior organization may indeed constitute a "socialism from below."[34] Submerge oneself within unions, the most organized working-class institutions, and build a communist project through unionism. One does not have to care very much about Draper (after all, he was so disconnected from social struggles in his own time that his thoughts on revolutionary practice should be treated as laughable) to accept something akin to the practice he advocated. Social unionism as part of an unquestioned insurrectionary strategy, albeit usually a movementist one, is one of the valid communist practices at the centres of capitalism.

The liquidation of communist practice amongst union activists, however, has tended to produce a phenomenon that was once called *economism*, where the necessity of communism is replaced by an activism determined by the need to promote the union's ability to secure its members' economic stability. Revolutionary necessity thus becomes hampered by immediate economic necessity. The late Action Socialiste, a Quebecois revolutionary project that peaked in the 1990s, has assessed its own experience with economism in the following manner:

---

34. See Hal Draper's *The Two Souls of Socialism* (http://www.marxists.org/archive/draper/1966/twosouls/index.htm). As noted earlier, Draperism has enjoyed a small resurgence. Following the anti-globalization movement, it is an early example of marxists attempting to fit themselves into the movementist discourse.

The whole organization was deeply affected by what we called 'economism:' spontaneous intervention within immediate (economic) struggles, abandoning agitation, propaganda and communist organizing. Economism is a form of right-wing opportunism; for its proponents, the movement represents everything, while the final goal (communism) no longer means anything. In [pursuing economism], we neglect to develop the revolutionary camp, and begin to abandon our most basic principles in order to achieve more immediate gains. [...] Several comrades then held leadership positions in student unions, community groups or workers' unions. The important goal for us at the time was to conquer the organizational leadership of mass movements. We sometimes got there, in some cases easily, because of our organizational talents. But this rarely meant ideological or political leadership. [...] What tends to happen in those times is either we put aside and 'hide' our real points of view (or even defend viewpoints we don't believe in), or we begin to develop bureaucratic practices to impose our minority viewpoints and keep the positions we attained in one movement or another.[35]

---

35. *Action Socialiste (1986-2000): An Unforgettable Experience* (Montreal: Maison Norman Bethune, 2009), 5.

Action Socialiste's experience is paradigmatic of trade-union activism on the part of communists; this economism is experienced, in greater or lesser degrees, by every communist who has sought to make union activism the basis of their revolutionary practice. If the situation was otherwise, after all, we would have long ago achieved the promise of Draperism: multiple red unions would have produced our revolutionary party. Instead, those of us who have attempted to find our communist way within union spaces should be able to recognize some of the claims made in the above quotation. Bogged down by collective agreements so that our activism becomes the management of union survival; fighting for a union leadership that is only marginally left in essence; finding ourselves on an executive or union working group that is politically divided; stranded in a union with people whose politics we despised, who were our "comrades" simply because they shared the same work space.

Every strike, no matter how radical, should remind us of the economist limits. Right when our immediate economic demands our met, regardless of those demands that challenge the economic system as a whole, we shut down the lines and go back to work—sometimes we end the strike even earlier, acceding to the strength of the employer in these times of austerity and because, in any case, we must keep the union alive.

Immediate economic demands, of course, are not insignificant. We have to put food on the table and pay the bills; we want job security and benefits. Solidarity amongst workers is laudable, and it would be a mistake to oppose unions and union drives because they are not as revolutionary as a communist party. The option, however, should never be the false dilemma of liquidating communist practice within the unions or opposing unionization on principle. To reject economism, to recognize that trade-unions, particularly at the centres of capitalism, may not be our primary spaces of organization should not produce a knee-jerk anti-unionism, no different in practice than the conservative hatred of unions; rather, it should cause us to recognize the necessity of focusing our organizational energies elsewhere. Without this recognition we end up conflating a practice limited by reformism with revolutionary agitation.

Hence, the mistake is to veil these immediate demands, which amount to a level of survival that is possible because of an organized workplace, with the trappings of communism. Revolutionary consciousness demands more than a consciousness determined by immediate demands, which is why today it is more likely to be found amongst the non-unionized workers who have not, through union economism, been integrated with the system. We cannot find, as a general rule, the worker with "nothing left to lose" in first world trade-unions. These unionized workers have much to lose, in the sense of immediate economic privileges, if they were to ever succeed in painting their union red—which is why, of course, it does not happen. Not now, not at the centres of capitalism.

the imaginative lack of imagination

In the previous chapter we confronted those theories that attempted reclamations of the name communism, that were little more than collaborations with the current state of affairs due to their unwillingness to grapple with the concrete situation. To take recourse in fantasy, to divorce themselves from struggle and pretend that imagination itself is struggle: in actuality, this is an ironic demonstration of a limited imagination. Regardless of one's creative feats in theoretical fantasy, the relegation of the question of organization and strategy to the possibility of spontaneity is rather uncreative; to assume that communism will just happen at distant point x based on our grandiose assertions and the combination of social movements is rather bland.

So what, then, do these reclamations tell us about reviving an anti-revisionist and revolutionary tradition if we are not to endorse the traps of bourgeois elections, refoundationalism, or economism? In their inability to creatively grapple with necessity we might be able to learn something significant—namely, how not to think.

Tiqqun's *Theory of Bloom* is a paradigm-example of this imaginative lack of imagination. After a whirlwind of theoretical eclecticism (from Debord to Baudrillard to Agamben—and all through Joyce!) they assert the name of the collective under which they would write their next movementist best-seller:

> The Invisible Committee: an *openly secret* society, a public conspiracy, an instance of anonymous subjectivation, whose name is everywhere and headquarters nowhere, the experimental-revolutionary polarity of the Imaginary Party. The Invisible Committee: not a revolutionary *organization*, but a higher level of reality, a metaphysical territory of secession with all the magnitude of a whole world of its own, the *playing area* where positive creation *alone* can accomplish the great emigration of the economy from the world.[36]

---

36. Tiqqun, *Theory of Bloom* (http://theanarchistlibrary.org/library/tiqqun-bloom-theory.pdf), 52.

Very imaginative language to simply conclude that there is no point in building a militant and organized movement in the real world. After all, how can one organize a mystical blanquist society that operates primarily upon a metaphysical terrain? The solution is to hope such a chimera can emerge spontaneously, through our creative play, which of course means that our only responsibility is to write and read theory, or at most embark on great acts of literary and artistic production.

And yet someone (or some people) decided that it was worth speaking in the name of this mystical organization, despite its impossibility of actually existing, because five years later we were given *The Coming Insurrection* by the Invisible Committee. Although there is something more concrete in the Invisible Committee's unflinching reclamation of the name communism, it is reclaimed only insofar as to appropriate it from an ideological tradition it despises—indeed, it refers to those Marxist-Leninists who developed the term historically as its enemies.[37] More importantly, though, is the fact that the Invisible Committee relies on an hazy understanding of the theory of insurrection, a strategy that has only met with failure after the October Revolution, but cleansed of its Leninism. Spontaneous insurrections without the wretched business of a civil

---

37. The Invisible Committee, *The Coming Insurrection*, 18.

war, and the assumption that the military and police forces will be won over by the fraternization of insurrectionists—because "[t]he *militarization* of civil war is the defeat of insurrection."[38] Necessity is denied merely on the assumption that the state's armed bodies of women and men will not violently put down untrained insurrectionists, that they will be politically won over by the insurrection itself. But the state has and will put down insurrections, and every insurrection since 1917 has indeed been violently suppressed—why pretend otherwise? Because we do not want to think through the hard questions demanded by necessity.[39]

The Uprising, by Franco Berardi, veritably shudders in its attempt to hide from the fact of revolutionary necessity: here the revolution is not even something that *happens* in a concrete sense, that has to do with unavoidable social truths. Ignored are the facts that there are armies trained to control

---

38. Ibid., 129.

39. All the furor surrounding the Tarnac 9, the supposed anarcho-communist cell responsible for writing *The Coming Insurrection*, was hype created by the French state. Even the bourgeois press agrees that the arrestees were not responsible for the conspiracy claimed by the French authorities; the defendants are not the "Baader-Meinhofs" the state hoped to discover insofar as they have denied the charges, thus claiming to be innocent of revolutionary activity. The arrests manifested as a publicity stunt, the state's attempt to spread the fear of home-grown terrorism amongst its citizenry.

populations, weapons monopolized by the ruling class, and a coercive state apparatus that will not deign to avoid a blood-bath when it is challenged. Rather, Berardi's revolution is something that happens in the imagination, a linguistic phenomena, the business of poetry.[40] Since the best satire is delivered with a straight face, it is tempting to speculate on whether or not Berardi is being serious or lampooning other chic social theories. After all, in the face of entire populations who are even now being bombed and occupied—these everyday massacres that are part of the normative operation of the flows of "finance" Berardi examines—to seriously suggest a linguistic and poetic revolution that is neither violent nor non-violent is tantamount to spitting in the face of the wretched of the earth and telling them that they should resist by writing poetry.

To the above three examples we can add the theories of "communization" promoted by Théorie Communiste and Endnotes. Influenced by, but critical of, the left/libertarian communism of Gilles Dauvé and *Socialisme ou Barbarie*, they peddle a theory that is yet another example of the same movementist practice with a communist mask.[41]

---

40. Franco "Bifo" Berardi, *The Uprising: on poetry and finance* (Los Angeles: Semiotext(e), 2012), 21-22.

41. In *Normative History and the Communist Essence of the Proletariat* (http://endnotes.org.uk/en/th-orie-communiste-

The problem for Théorie Communiste is the "programmatism" of the past cycles of revolution, cycles they think are finished.[42] While we should agree that there are different cycles of revolution, historical moments of continuity-rupture, it is notable that these communization theorists are incapable of thinking through the cycles of struggles unleashed by the Chinese Revolution, aside from dismissing it as "programmatic", let alone the contemporary cycles of struggles demonstrated by a storm of people's wars that began in 1988, mentioned at the outset of this treatise.

One might as well be a revisionist and an open collaborator with capitalism and imperialism to abide by the logic of these theoretical reclamations of the name communism. Even if those who limit their reclamation to a vague talk of hypotheses and horizons refuse to go this far down the road of a supposedly new communist imaginary, this is the terrain into which their trajectory falls. In the past these speculations were utopian, but to be utopian

---

normative-history-and-the-communist-essence-of-the-proletariat), Théorie Communiste in fact argues against the way in which Dauvé, despite reservations, still upholds the Russian Revolution and the importance of proletarian struggle.

42. For more information on this theoretical approach, the debates are contained within *Endnotes 1* (http://endnotes.org.uk/issues/1) and *Endnotes 2* (http://endnotes.org.uk/issues/2).

now, after so many earth-shaking revolutions where-in the masses won almost as much as they lost, is to plummet into the revisionist abyss—to wait in hope of spontaneity while, in the meantime, practicing a peaceful coexistence with this brutal reality.

The solution, however, is indeed imagination and creativity. But not a groundless imagination and creativity that cannot think through concrete problems, that reifies the current state of affairs. No, what we need is the kind of imagination and creativity that we find in the other sciences—imagining a future, and creatively building this future, based upon the truths won through past struggles. The history of successful or nearly successful revolutions and people's wars are instances in which revolutionary unity, however temporarily, was actually built. This is a past which radiates multiple necessities, the most important of which is communism.

We can predict, however, the way in which some of these theorists will respond to an analogy of scientific truth: they will remind us of the dangers of techno-scientific rationality and the totalizing nightmare of scientific progress. Since we addressed this complaint earlier, there is no reason to defend scientific necessity here. Instead, let us engage with these theories' lack of imagination according to the history of imagination and creativity itself—the history of literature, music, and the arts that is treated as significant, for example, by the Tiqqun group.

In the universe of creativity, the unreflective repetition of previous artistic production is usually understood as unremarkable. If we were to encounter an artist, unaware of the history of their craft, posturing as original while reproducing Duchamp's work in the early 20th century, we would treat them as arrogant and barely worthy of consideration. We know there is a history to literature and art that might teach us something, and this is the basis of any thoughtful judgment made in the terrain of imagination. Even Tiqqun believes that there is merit to this kind of judgment, if only implicitly; there is a reason it chooses to reference James Joyce rather than Dan Brown, Paul Valéry rather than Robert Frost, that is not reducible to literary elitism.

What do these theories offer, then, even according to the general standards of creative quality? The same movementist spontaneity, the same vague insurrection, the same distant horizon. Eclecticism is barely imaginative; it is about as creative as an elementary school collage. And in this eclectic mobilization of theory that is only imaginative in appearance there is a return to all of the utopian mistakes of the past.

new returns

To speak of a communist necessity is to also speak, in every particular situation in which a universalized communist theory might be articulated, of concrete praxis. And since talk of hypotheses, possibilities, horizons, produces a return to an ineffective movementism, how can we recognize a *new return* to an organized and totalized revolutionary practice when such a return is supposedly forbidden by the failures of actually existing socialism? This is the question, unfortunately, that is posed at the centres of capitalism where the word communism, after decades of suppression, is finally re-emerging.

Against this fad of reclaiming a name to which is attached a dubious concept, we assert that a single revolutionary programme that emerges from a concrete analysis of a concrete situation on behalf of a dynamic movement is worth more than a thousand academic marxist books or a thousand eclectic neo-communist theories. If communism is a necessity, then we cannot accept abstract reclamations that cannot grasp the need to make it a reality. We need to demand the concrete, we need to focus on literature produced by movements that are active in class struggle and, due to this activity, have also produced a theory that is itself generated by the necessities of struggle.

Nor can we ignore the fact that revolutionary communism was already reclaimed, right at the moment of the collapse of actually existing socialism, in the people's war in Peru, in the birth of the Revolutionary Internationalist Movement, in the launching of the people's war in Nepal, in the current people's war in India. These movements have spoken the name of communism, despite failure and setbacks, without ameliorating themselves in some inchoate movementism. Why they have been mostly ignored by the current intellectual fad of reclaiming the once-banned name is worth considering. Why self-proclaimed communists become annoyed when some of us speak of these actual revolutionary movements, complaining that they have heard enough about people's wars, and yet become excited with every doomed uprising or moribund populism, should make us wonder.

In many ways this excitement over banal movementist strategies represents a return to the utopian communisms that Marx and Engels once expended so much energy combatting in order to place the practice of making revolution upon scientific foundations. Indeed, Engels' focus on necessity represents this attempt to break from utopian idealism so that the pursuit of revolution would be more than an idle dream, a post-political hallucination. The errors of history are not so easily silenced and there will always be new returns to utopian anti-capitalism for as long as capitalism remains hegemonic. Unlike the so-called hard sciences, where previous paradigms are only endorsed by a minority of people who are generally understood as backwards, the science of revolution is a messy affair where innumerable dead-ends are preserved as vestigial philosophies that masquerade as science.

So in the face of the nightmare of capitalism, it is often tempting to resist with idle dreams of a utopian horizon and pretend that these dreams, as philosophically attractive as they sometimes might seem, are akin to revolutionary science. Often it is even more tempting to discard the terminology of science altogether, adopting philosophical skepticism, for it is quite dangerous for those who wish to avoid the problems of necessity to accept that revolution and history can be treated scientifically. Indeed, in these days where totality is seen as suspect and contingency has become a standard of theoretical labour, the speaking of *science* is often treated as an act of bad faith. Better to speak only of philosophy unmoored from the totalizing confines of science and thus plunge back into the philosophical socialism of the nineteenth century: utopianism.

The problem with this new return to utopianism is that those most taken with such an approach to communism often believe that they are indeed engaged in something *new*; the amnesia intrinsic to this idealism prevents them from realizing that it is also a *return*. They are quite willing to accept that they are returning to the name of communism but unwilling to accept that their manner of speaking this name—the fetishistic search for a new revolutionary strategy—is a return to a species of communism that, as Marx and Engels recognized, is incapable of manifesting revolution because it is incapable of recognizing its own necessity.

Thus there can be no absolute "dustbin of history," not until communism emerges, because we will always return, often in new ways, to the flawed ideas of yesteryear just as our enemy also remobilizes and rearticulates the reactionary ideologies of the past. As Marx noted, just when we assume we are engaged in revolutionizing ourselves, "in creating something that has never yet existed, precisely in such periods of revolutionary crisis [we] anxiously conjure up the spirits of the past."[43] The trick, however, is to discover what historical spirits we are conjuring, what masks we are donning, and that we are even donning them in the first place. Otherwise we run the risk of farcical historical repetition; these repetitions have already happened and are happening again.

Whereas the old communist utopianism spoke of "kingdoms of reason" and imagined emancipatory

---

43. Karl Marx, *The 18th Brumaire of Louis Bonaparte* (New York: International Publishers, 1969), 15.

social systems that, divorced from material and social relations, "the more they were completely worked out the more they could not avoid drifting off into pure phantasies,"[44] this new utopianism has drifted further into fantasy by hypothesizing a distant horizon that we could possibly and nebulously reach on one apocalyptic day. Now we have a utopianism that remains utopian about the practical means of achieving its fantasy while, at the same time, occasionally declaring fidelity to Marx or even Lenin.

This utopianism is a new return because its manifestation can be observed in all of the spontaneist currents of the early 20th century that attempted to distinguish themselves from the theory of a militant and vanguard revolutionary party by arguing for the self-organization of the working class. Although the utopian communists of today might claim that they know where the Leninist model of organization leads (to Stalin, to the gulags, to totalitarianism), they are often unreflective of the movementist model that has never succeeded in placing us on the road to revolutionary upheaval. The former model, regardless of its eventual failure, brought us closer to the supposed horizon of communism; the latter produced the rationale for tailing disarticulated

---

44. Friedrich Engels, *Socialism: Utopian and Scientific* (New York: International Publishers, 1998), 36.

mass movements in the name of a horizon these movements were not even trying to reach. So if we must have a new return to the past's revolutionary processes, then we should be aware of what process was the larger failure: the utopian theories of self-organization that led nowhere or the concrete theories of organized revolutionary necessity that produced world historical revolutions that, with all their errors, still shook the foundations of bourgeois reality? In thinking through this question we should be led to recognize that today's utopianism amounts to making social peace with capitalism.

Unfortunately, those who are committed to this resurgent utopianism would argue that a new return to the communism that developed through the path of necessity is also, and can only be, tragic and farcical. Despite the return to the name of communism, this new utopianism, due to its emergence in the heart of left-wing academia and petty-bourgeois student movements, has absorbed the post-modern fear of those who speak of a communist necessity—the fear of that which is totalizing and thus *totalitarian*. The failure to develop any concrete strategy of overthrowing capitalism, instead of being treated as a serious deficiency, is apprehended as a *strength*: the movement can be all things for all people, everything for everyone, everywhere and nowhere, "for when 'we' are truly everywhere, we will be nowhere—for we will be everyone."[45] But where did this utopianism lead; where can it lead? Nowhere, obviously, which was not the same as everywhere. These nebulous proposals sound nice, might even be more enjoyable to read than a party programme produced by a coherent revolutionary movement, but they are devoid of the strategy necessary for making a sustainable existence beyond the limits of capitalism a reality.

What is interesting about this new return to utopian communism, however, is that it has somehow succeeded in veiling itself in a praxis (or, due to movementist spontaneism, lack of praxis) that, by the 1990s, was considered the province of an anarchism and anti-capitalism that saw communism as a great mistake. In the days leading up to Seattle, at the heart of global imperialism, those who spoke of refusing to take power, of some new movement that could spontaneously end capitalism upon reaching a critical mass, and of the political fantasy described (but, of course, not prescribed) in *We Are Everywhere* would have eschewed the word "communism" since it stank of failure and totalitarianism and everything they were taught to despise in bourgeois high school textbooks. Now the word communism is being spoken into these spaces and, though a forbidding name, those who speak it are attempting to reconfigure the

45. *We Are Everywhere*, 511.

concept. Even the Invisible Committee, that imagines its own fantastical horizon of a coming insurrection without a Leninist party, has remobilized the word communism when, only decades earlier, the same people probably would have been made anxious whenever it was spoken.

In the face of this utopianism, then, it is important to argue instead for a new return to the revolutionary tradition that treated communism as a necessity. Not simply a dogmatic reassertion of something Lenin said in 1917, or something Marx said in 1848, but a return to the living science of this communism that originates with Marx and Engels, loops through Lenin, twists through Mao, and is still open to the future. All returns are always new, as Lenin learned when he creatively applied marxism to his social context, as Mao learned when he creatively applied marxism-leninism to his social context, as those of us who understand that communism must be understood as a necessity are trying to learn when we return to these past developments of necessity with a perspective that is always new because society changes... but also a return because society is burdened by the weight of dead generations.

Such a return must be concrete, must be able to speak the history of universal revolutionary necessity into each and every particular context in which we live and struggle. It is meaningless to only return to a name—to an uncritically inherited method of struggle that derives from a focus on vague hypotheses and horizons—unless we are willing to pursue everything this name came to mean over the course of revolutionary struggle since Marx. For when we return anew, over and over, to the necessity of making communism we will be confronted with great difficulties and the always immanent potential of failure. So much still needs to be accomplished.

Let us advance the struggle for making communism a concrete reality, and let us cease this prattle about some ideal communism that exists outside of time and space and instead, with all of the messiness this would imply, return to the recognition that its necessity requires a new return to the revolutionary communist theories and experiences won from history.

coda

Reality being what it is, the questions raised by this treatise are unlikely to be solved soon. If there is new return to the problematic of necessity, and a new anti-revisionist epoch of struggle replaces today's tired movementism, there is still the chance that only new failures will be encountered in the course of establishing new successes. We might succeed in temporarily breaching the distant communist horizon only to be catastrophically wrenched back into the nightmare of the present. The importance of necessity might again be forgotten, communism relegated once more to the realm of failure only to be yet again reclaimed by another new left that is even more wary of thinking of communism.

We should wonder how many repetitions are even possible; the window in which we can make revolution is closing as the world approaches the armageddon promised by the logic of capital. The fact of historical necessity is more visceral today than it has ever been. We cannot wait for a spontaneous arrival of the communist horizon when capitalism is nearing its own horizon—environmental collapse, a new ice age, the devastation of human existence as we know it—promised by its necessary and day-to-day operations. We cannot afford to tinker with its framework in the hope that the questions of revolution will be solved at some unknown point in the future. We cannot afford to waste our time in spaces and practices premised on the continuation of a system of exploitation, commodification, and eternal war.

Here, at the centres of capitalism, it is sometimes easy to banish the contemporary nightmare to the limbo regions of thought. While we may understand the logic of capitalism in theory, the gap between theory and practice often prevents us from embracing activity that is driven by the logic of revolutionary necessity. The contradictions of the system are more apparent in the peripheries; at the centres they are muted by a "culture industry" that persists only because of the most brutal exploitation and oppression elsewhere. Is it any wonder that the imperialist camp's longest war—the War on Terror—is not even experienced as a war by the masses who live at the centres of capitalism? Some of us have grown to adulthood with this war serving as an early childhood memory and yet, unlike those who have grown up in regions such as Afghanistan, have been able to live without experiencing the most direct and brutal affects of what George W. Bush once called, without irony, "the task that never ends."

From its very emergence, capitalism has waged war upon humanity and the earth. The communist necessity radiates from this eternal war: capitalism's intrinsic brutality produces an understanding that its limits must be transgressed, just as it produces its own grave-diggers. How can we be its grave-diggers, though, when we refuse to recognize the necessity of making communism concretely, deferring its arrival to the distant future? One answer to this problem is that those of us at the centres of capitalism are no longer the primary grave-diggers.

The permanent war capitalism wages upon entire populations is a war that is viscerally experienced by those who live at the global peripheries. Lenin once argued that revolutions tend to erupt at the "weakest links," those over-exploited regions where the contradictions of capitalism are clear. Thus, it should be no surprise that communism remains a necessity in these spaces—it is at the peripheries we discover people's wars. Conversely, opportunism festers at the global centres, these imperialist metropoles where large sections of the working-class have been pacified, muting contradictions and preventing entire populations from understanding the necessity of communism. Capitalism is not as much of a nightmare, here; it is a delirium, a fever dream.

Simply recognizing the current situation, however, is not enough. Often, such a recognition embraces the very opportunism it claims to critique. A recognition of opportunism that is opportunism itself: we cannot make revolution here, there are no cracks in which to build a militant organization capable of fighting capitalism at the global centres, we might as well wait upon the revolutionary labour of those comrades in the global south to save the world for us—we will embrace opportunism by declaring it an immutable fact! Again, the horizon is placed beyond our reach; breaching its limits is the business of others.

Communism is no longer an historical necessity if we fail to transgress the limits set by capitalism and are instead catapulted into the post-apocalyptic nightmare promised by the latter's intrinsic logic. In such a terrible event, if humanity survives only to find itself in another ice-age or devastated wasteland, it will encounter other necessities that are similar to the necessities encountered in the pre-capitalist past: how to persist as a species, how to build sustainable societies, how to produce historical memory. There will not be an eternal communist hypothesis when our existence is determined instead by more immediate questions of survival.

The necessity of communism is immediate now. In order to bring this necessity into being, though, we must learn to accept what has been established through every past, earth-shaking revolution that has also attempted to push beyond the boundaries set by capitalism. It may be the case that, in one sense, communism is the permanent dream of everyone who lives in a world strangled by capitalism, though a nightmare for the ruling classes. In another sense, however, we should stop thinking about communism solely as a dream, a fantastic horizon, and instead understand the ways in which past movements have temporarily made this dream concrete, briefly but significantly succeeding because they reversed the terms of dreaming: capitalism is the nightmare, communism the awakening. Often we would prefer to dream because it is easier; waking is never pleasant, especially in the early morning when, upon opening our eyes, we realize we have to go to work, clean our homes, raise our children, and deal with a host of concrete responsibilities — necessities — that we could forget while we dreamed.

Hence, communism should be approached as an awakening. In shaking off the nightmare of capitalism, the dreamers will also be shaken by the arduous tasks they must accomplish. Once again, as Mao reminds us, revolution is not a dinner party — nor is it a dream, a utopia, an eternal hypothesis, a distant horizon. But it is a necessity that is growing more immediate every year capitalism persists, a necessity that might vanish if and when capitalism's death throes obliterate existence.

In Borges' story, *Pierre Menard Author of the Quixote* we are introduced to a fictional author, Pierre Menard, who set himself the task of reproducing Cervantes' *Don Quixote*, not "another *Quixote*—which is easy—but *the Quixote itself*."[46] Rather than a rewriting of the same story in modern times, a reinvention of the proverbial Quixotic wheel, Menard ends up producing passages that are identical to the passages of Cervantes' original. And yet, as the narrator informs us, reproduction is impossible despite the word-for-word duplication; the different historical contexts in which the same passages are composed changes the meaning of both form and content. He concludes that Menard's version of the *Quixote*, though at first glance a reproduction of the original, is superior.

Similarly, whereas movementism demands a modern rewriting of the story of communism, we should demand a reproduction that is at the same time not a reproduction. By rearticulating the theoretical weapons of the past *now*, by creatively reasserting universality in today's particular instances, we will remember everything we were taught to

---

46. Jorge Luis Borges, *Labyrinths: Selected Stories & Other Writings* (New York: New Directions, 1964), 39.

forget. And in this remembering, painful as it might be, we will find ourselves standing on the shores of necessity.

acknowledgments

All books are ultimately the result of complex social processes in which, behind the author who signs his name to the project, there are innumerable other authors and voices. Beyond acknowledging this unavoidable fact of history, there are several people who directly contributed to the final version of this book. First of all, I need to thank Dhruv Jain and K. at Kersplebedeb who provided some content edits and suggestions. Secondly, I'm thankful for the work of Tyler Shipley whose copy-editing, as well as a few last second content suggestions, were invaluable. Finally, and most importantly, I am deeply thankful for the initial, substantial, and extremely significant editing and debating that my partner, Vicky Moufawad-Paul, contributed. Her lively, and sometimes wonderfully intense, discussions around the draft manuscript, not to mention all of the sections she convinced me to cut or rewrite, made this book far better than it would have been otherwise. I would not have been able to complete this project without her support.

about the author

J. Moufawad-Paul lives in Toronto and works as casualized contract faculty at York University where he received his PhD in philosophy. He shares a living space with his partner, Vicky, a brilliant artist and curator, and his daughter, Samiya, who will invariably lead the revolution once she realizes that her *Moomin* books do not count as revolutionary theory. J. Moufawad-Paul regularly blogs at *MLM Mayhem!*

about the kalikot book series

V.I. Lenin famously wrote that, "without revolutionary theory there can be no revolutionary movement." However, such a revolutionary theory adept at solving the theoretical problems faced by the contemporary revolutionary left has been largely unforthcoming or unavailable. Additionally, due to a prevalent Eurocentrism in North American and European radical traditions, books by or about Third World revolutionaries and their movements remain often unheeded and dismissed.

This book series hopes to publish the work of theoreticians and activists from around the world, not only the Third World, who advocate a wide variety of marginalized revolutionary politics. These are books that seek to serve as interventions into numerous complicated problems faced by the contemporary revolutionary left and to not only educate, but to help forge a revolutionary movement capable of the tasks before it.

For more information visit:

kalikotbooks.wordpress.com

ALSO FROM KERSPLEBEDEB

**The Worker Elite:
Notes on the "Labor Aristocracy"**

by Bromma

ISBN: 978-1-894946-57-5

88 pages • $10.00

Revolutionaries often say that the working class holds the key to overthrowing capitalism. But "working class" is a very broad category—so broad that it can be used to justify a whole range of political agendas. The Worker Elite: Notes on the "Labor Aristocracy" breaks it all down, criticizing opportunists who minimize the role of privilege within the working class, while also challenging simplistic Third Worldist analyses.

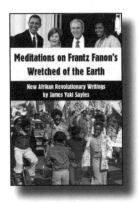

Meditations on Frantz Fanon's Wretched of the Earth: New Afrikan Revolutionary Writings

by James Yaki Sayles

ISBN: 978-1-894946-32-2

399 pages • $20.00

One of those who eagerly picked up Fanon in the 60s, who carried out armed expropriations and violence against white settlers, Sayles reveals how, behind the image of Fanon as race thinker, there is an underlying reality of antiracist communist thought. "This exercise is about more than our desire to read and understand Wretched (as if it were about some abstract world, and not our own); it's about more than our need to understand (the failures of) the anti-colonial struggles on the African continent. This exercise is also about us, and about some of the things that We need to understand and to change in ourselves and our world."—James Yaki Sayles

ALSO FROM KERSPLEBEDEB

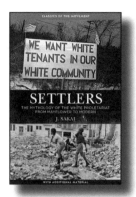

Settlers: The Mythology of the White Proletariat from Mayflower to Modern

by J. Sakai

ISBN: 978-1-62963-037-3

456 pages • $20.00

J. Sakai shows how the United States is a country built on the theft of Indigenous lands and Afrikan labor, on the robbery of the northern third of Mexico, the colonization of Puerto Rico, and the expropriation of the Asian working class, with each of these crimes being accompanied by violence. In fact, America's white citizenry have never supported themselves but have always resorted to exploitation and theft, culminating in acts of genocide to maintain their culture and way of life. This movement classic lays it all out, taking us through this painful but important history.

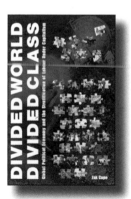

Divided World Divided Class: Global Political Economy and the Stratification of Labour Under Capitalism

by Zak Cope

ISBN: 9781894946414

385 pages • $20.00

This book demonstrates not only how redistribution of income derived from super-exploitation has allowed for the amelioration of class conflict in the wealthy capitalist countries, it also shows that the exorbitant "super-wage" paid to workers there has meant the disappearance of a domestic vehicle for socialism, an exploited working class. Rather, in its place is a deeply conservative metropolitan workforce committed to maintaining, and even extending, its privileged position through imperialism.

KER SPL EBE DEB

Since 1998 Kersplebedeb has been an important source of radical literature and agit prop materials.

The project has a non-exclusive focus on anti-patriarchal and anti-imperialist politics, framed within an anticapitalist perspective. A special priority is given to writings regarding armed struggle in the metropole and the continuing struggles of political prisoners and prisoners of war.

The Kersplebedeb website provides downloadable activist artwork, as well as historical and contemporary writings by revolutionary thinkers from the anarchist and communist traditions.

Kersplebedeb can be contacted at:

> Kersplebedeb
> CP 63560
> CCCP Van Horne
> Montreal, Quebec
> Canada
> H3W 3H8
>
> email: info@kersplebedeb.com
> web: www.kersplebedeb.com
>   secure.leftwingbooks.net